Successful Project Sponsorship

A time-saver for the busy executive

Michiel van der Molen

KoganPage

LONDON PHILADELPHIA NEW DELHI

First published in Great Britain and the United States in 2015 by Kogan Page Limited

2nd Floor, 45 Gee Street	1518 Walnut Street, Suite 1100	4737/23 Ansari Road
London EC1V 3RS	Philadelphia PA 19102	Daryaganj
United Kingdom	USA	New Delhi 110002
		India

www.koganpage.com

© Michiel van der Molen, 2015

The right of Michiel van der Molen to be identified as the author of this work has been asserted by him in accordance with the Copyright, Designs and Patents Act 1988.

ISBN   978 0 7494 7424 9
E-ISBN 978 0 7494 7425 6

British Library Cataloguing-in-Publication Data

A CIP record for this book is available from the British Library.

Library of Congress Cataloging-in-Publication Data

Molen, Michiel van der.
    Successful project sponsorship : a time-saver for the busy executive / Michiel van der Molen.
        pages cm
    ISBN 978-0-7494-7424-9 (paperback) – ISBN 978-0-7494-7425-6 (ebk)
1. Project management. I. Title.
    HD69.P75M66 2015
    658.4'04—dc23
                                                                                    2015016004

Typeset by Amnet
Print production managed by Jellyfish
Printed and bound by CPI Group (UK) Ltd, Croydon, CR0 4YY

CONTENTS

ABOUT THE AUTHOR

Michiel van der Molen MSc has experienced a wide range of projects in areas such as urban renewal, information technology and organizational change while working for local and central government and in manufacturing, retail, finance and education. He has filled the roles of project sponsor, project manager, management trainer and management consultant and has worked in the Netherlands, Germany, Belgium, the United Kingdom and Tanzania. As a co-founder of Molen & Molen he helps organizations to advance project governance, project sponsorship, business case development and benefits management. To find out more, go to his company website www.molenmolen.nl/en.

PREFACE

As a project manager, programme manager and project sponsor I have been involved in projects in a variety of sectors in several countries. Later in my career I was the manager of a team of project managers and, as such, responsible for projects for various customers. I learned that when a project is in trouble, issues related to project execution are often solvable: in the worst case by replacing the project manager. Issues related to project direction, however, are the most difficult to solve. These refer to the responsibilities of the project sponsor, such as taking care of a clear business case, timely decision-making and adequate empowerment of the project manager. Sometimes effective project sponsorship can be even more of a challenge than professional project management.

Driven by the need to better support our customers in performing their project sponsor roles I went in search of an easily readable book about project sponsorship and was surprised not to find it. In 2002 I decided to write this book myself, not realizing that this would fundamentally change my career.

The demand for the book – the Dutch version sold over 12,000 copies and keeps selling – showed that it fulfilled a need in a way that exceeded all my expectations. The demand for training, consultancy and lectures on project sponsorship soon enabled me to fully focus on what was to become my professional passion: supporting the advancement of project sponsorship in organizations and, in a wider sense, the deepening of business management engagement with projects through training and consultancy in the areas of project governance, project sponsorship, business case development and benefit management.

While many organizations striving to advance project performance still focus exclusively on the project manager's role and the corresponding procedures and methodology, my experience confirms that it is precisely the closer engagement of business management that speeds up and deepens the change process. I hope this book will contribute to this.

Advancing project sponsorship still is a relatively new area of expertise. I therefore invite anyone interested to share their questions, comments and ideas, through the LinkedIn group Project Sponsorship, through Twitter (#projectsponsorship) or privately through our company website: www.molenmolen.nl/en. I find it exciting that this book is now available for an international audience and I'm looking forward to learning from your reactions.

Michiel van der Molen

ACKNOWLEDGEMENTS

This book is an adaptation of a Dutch book, five editions of which have appeared since 2003. I owe many thanks to all the project sponsors, project managers and project management trainers who contributed with their guidance and feedback to one or more of these editions: Ad van den Akker, Martin de Boer, Paul Bogerd, Jos Dams, Brigit Darlang, Alette Faber, Herman Hanekamp, Dick La Haye, Wil Hendrickx, Arja Hilberdink, Peter Koers, Eva van der Molen, Hans van der Molen, Kim van Oorschot, Albert Peek, Henny Portman, Reynier Pronk, Sylvie Rath, Rob Schepens, Maarten Speet, Luc van Veggel, Wim Vleeskens and David E J Wilson.

When working on this edition, I had all the support I could have wished for. I thank Liz de Vries for her language advice. It is great to work with a native speaker of English who is also fluent in Dutch and so engaged to help me with all the language issues that arose when working on this edition. I thank Anton Zandhuis, co-author of *A Pocket Companion to PMI's PMBOK® Guide* and *ISO 21500 – A Pocket Guide* for his comments on the alignment of this book with the PMBOK. I thank Sander Hoogendoorn, author of *This is Agile*, for our inspiring discussions on agile project management and for his comments on the tips for agile projects and everything else that this book says about agile. I thank Ross Garland, author of *Project Governance*, for his expert comments on a draft version of the manuscript.

Part 3, about the advancement of project sponsorship in organizations, is new text, not contained in the original version of this book. I thank Corien Kiel, Eric Pieper and Luc van Veggel for their very useful comments.

Last but not least my thanks go to my publisher, Jennifer Hall, for taking the trouble to go into the work of a Dutch author, for putting her confidence in me and for giving the book a much better title and subtitle. I also thank my editor, Lucy Carter, for her valuable comments and suggestions.

As a result of the enthusiasm and engagement of all those supporting me, working on this book has been a truly joint effort and a very pleasant experience.

Introduction

The challenge

As a manager you have more than just operational responsibilities. Driven by developments in society, the economy, the market, technology and legislation you are also responsible for improving operating processes, developing new products, creating new services and bringing about other changes.

You decide to start a project. You want to delegate the daily management of this project to others, but the final accountability stays with you. This book shows you how to be successful in this role, to the benefit of your organization and its stakeholders.

Is it actually a project?

A project implies a separation of responsibilities: at the very least it takes a project manager and a project sponsor (also referred to as project executive or project owner). The first makes a plan and the second approves it. This will only be worthwhile when there is enough complexity and risk to justify this overhead. Sometimes the best thing is *not* to waste time on managing but to just *do* something. A rule of thumb is: if the standing organization is able to do it by itself, don't make it into a project.

> ### Project
>
> A project is a temporary endeavour undertaken to create a unique product, service or result (the project objective, a deliverable). The sponsoring organization starts a project in order to achieve a business goal (a positive effect for itself or its stakeholders).

A project approach is not suitable for all complex changes. It is useful to bring about a tangible result that is relatively predictable, such as a new building, a new version of a product or an adapted computer system. If the main challenge lies in a change of culture or behaviour, in the way that organizations work together, or when the success of the changes significantly depends on the support of external parties with conflicting interests, other approaches such as programme management are more likely to be suitable.[1]

What is a project sponsor?

A project sponsor is the pivot point between the permanent (line) organization and the temporary (project) organization. It is the person guiding the project manager on behalf of the standing organization, linking the project to corporate direction. The difference between the project sponsor and other stakeholders is that for a project sponsor the project is an investment. As a project sponsor you can only justify this investment when the benefits (whether financial or non-financial) offset the costs. Other stakeholders are not responsible for the investment decisions, although they do experience benefits (positive effects) or disbenefits (negative effects) as a result of the project.

> ### Project sponsor
>
> This is the single individual who is responsible on behalf of the (permanent) line organization to direct the (temporary) project organization, representing the business interests in the direction of the project and accountable for the realization of its business case.

As a project sponsor, when you decide to start a project, a lot of questions arise. This book provides answers to the following:

- How can I come to a clear definition of the project mandate, while the environment is permanently changing?
- How can I make stakeholders buy in to the goal of the project and contribute to it?
- How do I underpin the budget?
- What responsibilities do I give to the project manager?
- How do I assess a plan or a performance report?
- How do I control quality without getting lost in details?
- Why do so many projects end up going over budget and what can I do as a project sponsor to prevent this?
- How do I get the benefits realized?

Assumptions of this book

When do we call a project a success? When the project manager completes the project on time, within budget, and the project result meets the quality criteria? That is not enough. If the project deliverable is not properly used (in the broadest sense of the word – used, operated, managed, exploited, maintained, sold, bought, rented, inhabited and so forth) then the project was for nothing. Is it a success, then, if the project deliverable is accepted and used? From the project sponsor's perspective even more is needed. A project is an investment and an investment is something you do in order to realize certain benefits (positive effects, whether financial or not), for instance financial profit, social benefits or compliance to regulations. This is the business goal. Only when you achieve this can you call a project a success. Often it takes some time after completion of the project before you can determine if the business goal has been realized.

The accountability for the achievement of this business goal can only lie with the project sponsor. The project sponsor is responsible for the investment decision, for approving the plan, for appointing the project manager, for decision-making about changes to the plan and, more importantly, for getting the benefits realized. When a project fails, it is similar to other cases of failure in organizations, like fraud, ecological scandals or serious quality problems: business management (line management) is accountable. The assumptions of this book are therefore:

- A project is only successful if the business goal is achieved.
- The project sponsor, as a representative of line management, is accountable for the success of a project.

Some see the project sponsor as someone who should take care of the funding of the project and leave decision-making to the project manager as much as possible. If you are happy with that, then don't read this book. This book is for business managers who want to take responsibility for project direction and the realization of its benefits.

But what about the project manager?

The project manager's principal responsibility is to deliver the agreed project result, with the required quality, within the cost and time agreed. This is under the condition that the project sponsor maintains the agreed conditions such as availability of information and resources, access to buildings and installations, and timely decision-making.

This book is *not* a 'project management summary' and does *not* go into matters such as the composition of project teams or the control of specialist work. This book focuses on the principles that help you to give effective strategic direction from a business perspective, presuming that the daily management of the project is in the hands of a capable project manager. In case you have doubts about the latter, I would advise you to solve this issue first.

International standards

The terminology in this book is in line with the international Project Management Body of Knowledge (PMBOK®).[2]

In the United Kingdom and various other countries PRINCE2™ is the most popular project management method.[3] Where relevant, this book contains specific tips for the PRINCE2 environment.

Tip for the PRINCE2 environment

There are slight differences in terminology between this book and PRINCE2. The relevant ones are shown in Table 0.1.[4]

TABLE 0.1 Differences in terminology between this book and PRINCE2

PMBOK and This Book	PRINCE2
project sponsor	executive
steering group	project board
deliverable	product
project charter	project brief
project definition and planning	project initiation

Agile is a collective noun for a number of project approaches, defined in 2001 by a group of software development professionals. The essence of agile is that people are more important than processes and tools, and that rapidly and effectively reacting to change is more relevant than following a plan.

> **Tip for agile projects**
>
> In some aspects agile projects are the same as any project, in some aspects they are not. Throughout this book you will find tips for sponsors of agile projects on how to apply the general insights of this book to an agile project or to an agile part of a larger project.

How to read this book

Part 1 contains the foundation of this book: *the four principles of successful project sponsorship*. Part 2 can be read in any order for more detail and answers to practical questions on topics including the steering group, how to deal with the project manager, benefits, quality, changes, risk and assessing project documents. If you are involved in an initiative aiming at the organization-wide advancement of project sponsorship, read Part 3 for an outline approach and a number of practical tips.

Throughout the book you will find quotes from project sponsors I have worked with ('A project sponsor says…'), mostly confirming the content of this book but sometimes presenting a slightly different viewpoint – in real life there can be more than one answer to the same question.

The book concludes with appendices explaining the essence of the PMBOK, PRINCE2 and agile, and an appendix summarizing the responsibilities and accountabilities related to the direction and management of a project. In addition, an appendix about the terminology used in this book is included. There is a Glossary containing definitions of all professional terms used in this book and the most popular alternative terms.

Notes

1 For more information see *The Standard for Program Management* (PMI, 2013b) and *Managing Successful Programmes* (OGC, 2007).

2 For more information about PMBOK see *A Guide to the Project Management Body of Knowledge (PMBOK® Guide)* (PMI, 2013).

3 For more information about PRINCE2 see *Directing Successful Projects with PRINCE2™* (OGC, 2009).

4 The PRINCE2 terms listed are not necessarily exact synonyms, but in my opinion they are corresponding concepts.

PART ONE
Principles

Introduction to Part 1
The four principles of successful project sponsorship

More strategic control for less effort

Most project sponsors have two things in common. First, the feeling that they lack control to effectively direct their projects towards success. Second, given that their sponsor roles come on top of their operational responsibilities, the feeling that they lack time to improve this. This book helps you with both.

In the first instance, this book helps you to become more effective and allows you to get your projects to contribute to the achievement of your goals in the best possible way. In addition, this book helps you to become more efficient. This means that you make optimum use of the resources both inside and outside your organization, so that project sponsorship requires the minimum level of effort and leaves you sufficient room to pay attention to your other responsibilities.

Indeed I presume that you want more effectiveness and more efficiency, or in other words, more strategic control for less effort. This is what I have learned from surveys among participants of project sponsorship training programmes, conducted a few months after each training session to find out what the added value of the training was in real life.

Over the years, through continued revision to my training programmes in the light of direct feedback, I found that successful project sponsorship comes down to four proven principles, which are presented in Part 1. Each chapter finishes with a brief summary of how the principle contributes to the effectiveness and efficiency of project sponsorship. At the end of Part 1 you will find two summaries: a summary of the four principles discussed and a reverse summary: that is, a summary of what you might expect when you *don't* apply these four principles.

Common sense

Applying these four principles is not the only thing you have to do. Project sponsorship is a management activity, which implies adapting your behaviour to circumstances, guided not only by a book but by common sense – and at times just doing what has to be done. In doing so, the four principles will help you to focus on the essentials.

Four areas of attention

In the Introduction we discussed the difference between what the project manager delivers (the project objective, the immediate project result) and the effect for stakeholders (the project goal, the result at business level). As a project sponsor you are accountable for both, so you have to deal with these two levels, ensuring that the project result is aligned to the intended business result. But results are not the only thing to focus on. Results can only be achieved if many people are willing to make an effort. Indeed, you will need support in order to bring about change as you don't have all the knowledge yourself,

FIGURE 0.1 The four areas of consideration for the project sponsor

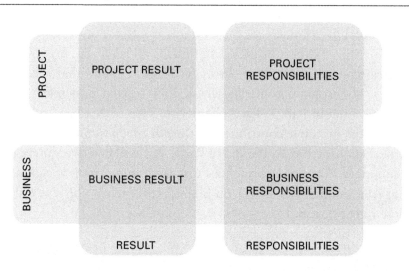

you have a full agenda and you want to use your time efficiently. This is why it is important to pay attention not only to the result, but also to the responsibilities. The more that people feel responsible for their contribution to this result, and the clearer the responsibilities are, the more they will be willing to create solutions and make an effort to achieve them, thus the greater the chance of success.

Therefore, the starting point of the four principles of successful project sponsorship is that at both levels – business and project – you focus on two aspects: result and responsibilities. This leads to four areas of consideration for the project sponsor, as presented in Figure 0.1.

The four principles

The four principles of successful project sponsorship each address one of the four areas of consideration, as presented in Figure 0.2:

- **The first principle**: the leading principle regarding the business result is *share the business case.*[1] This principle defines how to come to a shared understanding of the reasons behind (the why) and relevance of the project, so that stakeholders

FIGURE 0.2 The four principles of successful project sponsorship

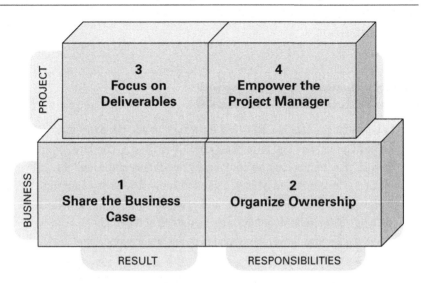

can connect with it, and how to use this as a foundation for all communication and decision-making.

- **The second principle**: the leading principle regarding business responsibilities is *organize ownership*. This principle defines how you can get stakeholders (such as members of the steering group or users) not only to connect with the goal of the project, but also to feel an individual responsibility to deliver a specific contribution to this goal.

- **The third principle**: the leading principle regarding the project result is *focus on deliverables*. This principle defines how to focus on deliverables as the backbone of the project, and how to use this to create transparency and control project realization, in order to get the project to deliver those tangible results that will enable you to achieve the intended business results.

- **The fourth principle**: the leading principle regarding the project responsibilities is *empower the project manager*. This principle defines how to direct the project manager and what control mechanisms (such as stages and reporting) to agree on in order to get the project result delivered against minimum effort, in a controlled way and with enough flexibility.

In addition to the general leadership qualities you need, these four principles can be seen as the building blocks of the leadership of the project sponsor.

Tip for the PRINCE2 environment

As a project sponsor in a PRINCE2 environment you need to know the basic principles and terminology of PRINCE2. The standard PRINCE2 Foundation course contains all the details of the method, which is a lot more than what you need to know. Effectively applying the four principles defined in this book – which fully support PRINCE2 – will help you more than getting into the details of the method.

Table 0.2 shows how the principles of this book support the principles of PRINCE2.

TABLE 0.2 Principles of successful project sponsorship and corresponding PRINCE2 principles

The Four Principles of Successful Project Sponsorship	Corresponding PRINCE2 Principles
1 – Share the business case	Continued business justification
2 – Organize ownership	Defined roles and responsibilities
3 – Focus on deliverables	Focus on products
4 – Empower the project manager	Manage by stages
	Manage by exception

Two PRINCE2 principles are not explicitly covered by this book: 'learn from experience' (a general management principle, highly relevant but not specific for project sponsorship) and 'tailor PRINCE2 to suit the project' (a principle focused on the application of the method itself).

Tip for agile projects

For successful sponsorship of agile projects the same principles apply, although their application is slightly different:

- *Share the business case* is fundamental to help the product owner and development team set the right priorities and make the right choices (see Chapter 1).

- *Organize ownership* is absolutely necessary to create the high level of user involvement needed for successful agile development (see Chapter 2).

- *Focus on deliverables* refers to the order and the scope of the work items in the product backlog (see Chapter 3).

- *Empower the project manager* may also be interpreted as 'empower the development team as a whole', as some agile projects do without a project manager (see Chapter 4).

Note

1 A business case is not merely a financial trade-off. It is the answer to the question why we do the project. The reasons behind a project may be financial and/or non-financial such as legal, health or safety.

The first principle: share the business case

FIGURE 1.1 The first principle

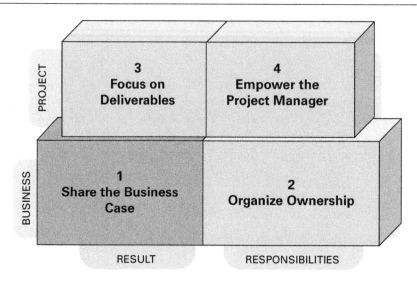

It's the business result that counts

We used to say: a project is a success when it delivers the planned project result, with the agreed quality, on time and within budget. But in the present increasingly dynamic world it is not enough any more to deliver at the end of the project what we had agreed at the beginning. It is normal that, in the course of the project, changes in the project environment force us to change our plan. Exceptions have become the rule, and project management has developed into aiming at moving targets. That is why we now say: a project is an investment, so it is only successful when it contributes to the objectives of the sponsoring organization. This principle is about the 'why' of the project.

Focus

Stephen Covey says: 'Begin with the end in mind' (Covey, 1989). In a project this is the role of the business case: an explanation of how the envisaged project will contribute to corporate objectives, taking into account costs, benefits and risks. It is the reason why the sponsoring organization starts the project in the first place, and you can use it to create focus in what people do. The more the stakeholders feel engaged with the business case of a project, the less you are dependent on subjective preferences, because you have a common frame of reference for decision-making, about the start of the project as well as later go/no-go decisions and changes. And the less likely it is that the project will take on a life of its own as a so-called construction project or ICT project (that is, perceived as mainly in the hands of a supplier) instead of a business project (with clear business ownership). In the end, each project is a business project.

A project sponsor says...

A CEO of an energy company, when confronted with the first principle (*share the business case*) in a project sponsorship workshop noted:

'But this is in contradiction with our culture.' When asked to explain more, he added: 'This would bring transparency into our decision-making.'

Project direction based on a business case indeed is not a matter of methodology. It may require a radical change of culture to put this into practice.

Basis for communication

Not only formal decision-making benefits from a clear business case. Also at operational level there is a great need for a shared vision. John Kotter pointed out the enormous value of a vision (Kotter, 1996). It provides guidance for and thus simplifies numerous more detailed decisions. It motivates people to move in the right direction and helps to overcome resistance, and it helps to efficiently coordinate the actions of large numbers of different people. A good business case articulates the vision behind the project and is guiding and motivating. Therefore you should use the business case not only as a frame of reference for formal decision-making, but also as a basis for all communication with stakeholders. This requires you to be able to summarize the business case briefly and powerfully.

One-liner

In order to get a project budget in a large organization, often all possible benefits of a project are enumerated, quantitative as well as qualitative ones, essential ones as well as nice-to-haves. What arises is a multiple business case, with various benefits such as shorter delivery times, improved efficiency, enhanced quality and improved image, and where possible quantified and added. This will serve well to underpin the budget request, but at the same time it may lead to confusion about the project's essence and will hinder effective communication with stakeholders: you always need a long story to explain the project and most likely everyone will tell the story in a different way. Therefore, the business case should not only enumerate all benefits, but should also clearly explain why you are undertaking the project. The core of a strong business case, suitable for daily communication, is a one-liner supported by the stakeholders. A clear business case fits on a beer mat.

The value of a clear business case [1]

A packaging company is working on a logistic improvement project. In the first phase of the project, the project sponsor invites the members of the steering group for a start-up meeting to lay a solid foundation for successful project direction. One of the first items on the agenda is an inventory of what, in the eyes of the participants, are the main bottlenecks in the project. One of the user representatives in the steering group sees as the main bottleneck the growing flow of issues that in this early phase of the project is already overwhelming her: 'The issues and change requests come in faster than we can decide on them. The list of open issues is only getting longer. We are drowning in it.'

The next item on the agenda is the business case. The business case document defines three benefits:

- reduced delivery times;
- increased flexibility for customers;
- reduced stock levels, hence cost reduction through reduced use of capital.

According to most steering group members the cost reduction through reduced stock levels is the main reason why the project started. After some discussion, however, the project sponsor states that in the end it's about service. As 80 per cent of the company's turnover comes from a small group of large customers, at corporate level the strategic choice had been made to align all business processes to the needs of these large customers in order to tighten the relationship with them and sustainably retain and develop their business. This is what the reduced delivery times and increased flexibility are needed for. The cost reduction appears to be an important additional benefit that enables the justification of the project to those who primarily look at the direct financial effect. But the main reason behind the project is to retain the best customers with the best service. The steering group comes to a summary of the business case in a one-liner: 'Tailor-made logistics in order to sustainably develop the business with our largest customers.'

Now that the essence of the business case is clear, they need to check if this helps to manage the increasing flow of issues. The steering group member who mentioned this bottleneck is asked to give an example of an annoying small issue that leads to a disproportionate discussion. 'For example a proposal to add one extra field on a computer screen', she explains. 'It is one of the screens our customers work with. We have been fighting over this for three weeks already.' The next question is what the issue would look like if it was looked at from the perspective of the essence of the business case: tailor-made logistics in order to sustainably retain the company's largest customers. 'Well, then it would be obvious', the member says. 'This single field is useful to manage exceptions. These exceptions are only relevant for our smaller customers, for which we use slightly different processes. Our larger customers don't need this field and for them it will only be confusing.'

Based on the essence of the business case, she draws the logical conclusion not to include this extra field. She looks at the project sponsor to check if there are any objections to applying the business case in this way. The project sponsor thinks it makes perfect sense: 'We are not going to optimize our processes to the wishes of smaller customers, they should be optimized for the large customers.'

Apparently, as soon as the business case was clarified, the issue was solved. Had the business case been clear from the beginning, the issue probably wouldn't even have been raised. Lack of clarity of the business case is a lack of leadership.

When communicating the business case to users, suppliers and other stakeholders, in the first place use this one-liner and keep repeating it. This is what you want everyone to remember. When necessary, use the full business case document to underpin the one-liner and to nuance it.

Tip for the PRINCE2 environment

PRINCE2 contains a detailed layout of a business case document. The risk of this is that developing a business case document becomes a specialist job. However, a brief and imperfect business case document developed with (and hence truly understood and supported by) the principle stakeholders might be of more value than a complete and theoretically perfect business case document written by a project manager or controller.

Business case categories

A business case does not necessarily have to be of a financial nature. Based on their business cases, projects can be divided into four groups:

- **Mandatory or unavoidable projects.** You undertake these because without them the organization cannot continue. In most cases they are driven by a legal obligation. Although it is hard to determine the financial value of the result, the business cases of these projects are cast iron: in reality the success rate of the projects based on them is nearly 100 per cent.

- **Continuity projects.** You undertake these to prevent too many breakdowns, or maintenance costs rising too high, or in order to mitigate other increasing risks. The basis for the investment decision is usually a risk assessment. If there is a large chance of limited damage occurring (like in the case of a continuity project aiming to reduce a steadily growing number of failures in a production process), then the business case can well be underpinned financially. If there is a very small chance of a serious disaster occurring, it is harder to come to an objective justification. In that case the decision will probably be more political, to be made at the highest level of the organization.

- **Enabler projects.** These are not directly focused on benefits, but you undertake them – sometimes as part of a programme – to enable other projects that do deliver benefits. If you wouldn't undertake these other projects, the enabler project has no value and therefore no justification. There is a business case, but it lies at a higher level and refers to a combination of projects.

- **Benefit-driven projects.** These projects focus directly on matters such as saving cost, increasing market share or improving health or safety. A strong business case is one that explicitly aligns with the organization's strategic objectives. If the main objective of an organization is financial, then financial arguments will be the strongest. When an organization (also) pursues other objectives, other arguments can be decisive. Strive for quantification of benefits, including when they are non-financial, to make the success of the project measurable and to allow alternative solutions to be compared.

Leadership

Creating a shared business case is the essence of the leadership of the project sponsor. This means: taking care that everyone understands why the project is being realized. It is a precondition for grass-roots support, stakeholder engagement and joint focus.

The business case is not a document

It is a common pitfall – supported by numerous templates and checklists that circulate over the internet – to confuse the development of a business case with the creation of a business case document. Developing a business case is developing support for an investment decision, and the business case is the reason to invest. This reason exists regardless if you put it into writing, though of course it is advisable to have the result of this process recorded in a business case document. Chapter 10 explains how to check a business case document.

How does a business case come about?

As a project sponsor, in most cases you don't have hierarchic power over all the stakeholders and you cannot achieve a joint focus with one-way communication. By involving stakeholders in formulating the business case you offer them the opportunity to connect with and buy in to the project. This might require a process of giving and taking: you might prefer an agreement on a business case that supports 80 per cent of your interests to a conflict about a business case that supports 100 per cent of your interests.

Be clear about why you want to start the project, what most essential benefits you want to achieve (financial or non-financial) and what aspects are absolutely non-negotiable. If you delegate the rest of the process of the business case development to a project manager, ensure that they involve the right stakeholders, internal (managers from departments involved, internal suppliers, risk specialists and controllers) as well as external (customers, partner organizations and suppliers).

Elaborating the technical aspects of a business case, such as return on investment (ROI) analysis, and drafting a business case document can be delegated to the project manager or a business case specialist, after having stated your key assumptions and constraints.

Stage transitions and changes

A clear business case provides a solid basis for setting priorities. Use the business case as a foundation for decision-making, not only at the start of the project, but also at stage transitions and change requests. In decision-making on a running project, don't use the original business case, but the most up-to-date one. What counts is that you come to a trade-off between costs still to be made (that is, excluding 'sunk costs') and benefits to be realized, taking into account current risks and the potential costs of premature closure of the project. When evaluating a change request the question is: which solution contributes most to the realization of the business case?

How is the business case maintained?

At the end of each project stage, before you give permission to proceed to the next stage, check if the business case is still valid. Market developments, changes in legislation, technological developments or growing insight within the project team can all be triggers to adjust the business case and redefine priorities. When changing the business case, in order to maintain stakeholder engagement, carefully consider engaging the same stakeholders who were involved in developing it. Of course, after having spent part of the budget on the past stage, there should be a new estimate of the costs still to be made.

Also, check the business case in the event of calamities and when evaluating change requests. Based on a current understanding of the business case and risk you might decide to continue the project without changes, to adjust it or to close it.

What to do if not everything runs according to plan

Even the most successful projects often do not run according to plan: they are successful precisely because in changing circumstances the plan is adjusted in a timely and appropriate way. Yet most project plans focus almost exclusively on 'what to do if everything runs according to plan' and pay little attention to 'what to do if *not everything* runs according to plan'. The pre-eminent foundation for efficient and effective project direction, in case not everything runs according to plan, is a clear and shared business case.

Yardstick for success

After completion of a project the sponsoring organization should learn from it. An important consideration is whether the planned results have been delivered to stated quality standards and within the cost and time agreed. Answers to this question may lead to conclusions regarding the capabilities of the project manager or supplier. An even more relevant yardstick, however, is an assessment based on the business case: to what extent has the project contributed to corporate objectives? Often this can only be determined after the project has been completed for some time and the first benefits have become visible.

Quality of business cases influenced by context

The way that an organization deals with business cases can be highly influenced by budget policies, and the extent to which project sponsors are held accountable for the realization of their business cases.

For example, a telecom provider annually approved only the strongest business cases based on a high standard for return on investment. The business cases submitted by the project sponsors were always extremely optimistic in order to get the budget, because they knew they were never held accountable for actually achieving their business case.

A public sector organization used to translate the expected financial savings mentioned in business cases directly into budget cuts for the next year. In order to avoid this, most project sponsors left the financial aspects of the business cases of their projects as vague as possible, referring to the social objectives of the organization.

Benefits realization

Of course you don't leave the realization of benefits to chance. Who feels responsible to realize the proposed benefits? Do they consider the realization of these benefits to be achievable with the aid of the products to be delivered by the project? These are important questions to ask during the development of a business case. After all, as long as these questions are not adequately met, a business case is non-binding and may be based on wishful thinking rather than the determination to achieve improvements. More on this can be read in Chapter 2 on the second principle: *organize ownership*.

Summary

The first principle, *share the business case*, gives direction to the efforts of all involved and helps them to connect with the project. It contributes to:

- strengthening the sponsorship of senior management;
- better support among stakeholders and hence more cooperation;
- therefore less problems with the supply of resources;
- less room for conflicts of interests between stakeholders;
- a continued focus on the intended business results instead of only the project results, so that the project will not take on a life of its own;
- fewer spurious debates about details arising because stakeholders have different views of the 'why';
- efficient use of resources through a clear focus, hence less waste;
- good anticipation of the project manager of steering group decision-making, enabling him or her to propose changes that reinforce the business case and to refrain from proposing changes that do not, thus improving the efficiency of steering group decision-making;
- at all levels: better decision-making on details based on a motivated trade-off between user and business interests.

In short, very little contributes as much to achieving positive business results as a clear and shared business case. The time you spend working with stakeholders on creating it will be more than worth it and most of the benefits mentioned above will save you a lot of time.

Note

1 Translated from 'Waarom doen we dit eigenlijk? De businesscase als succesfactor van projecten' (Why are we doing this? The business case as project success factor) (Van der Molen, 2013).

The second principle: organize ownership

FIGURE 2.1 The second principle

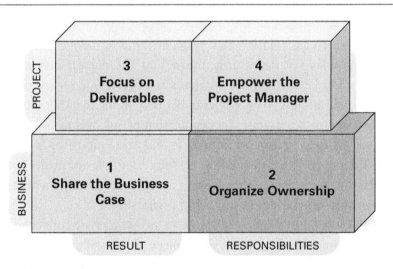

Business management is accountable for project success

A common pitfall is the idea that a good project manager is a guarantee for success. The project manager is responsible for the daily management of the project, but only business managers can be responsible for the direction of the project from a business perspective and for the realization of the proposed benefits. Therefore, the accountability for project success can only lie with business management. While the application of project management processes should be left to the project manager, the assignment of business management responsibilities around the project is very much your concern as a project sponsor – and that is what this principle is about. Subsequent topics in this chapter are: the responsibilities of the project sponsor, of other steering group members and other business management responsibilities.

This principle is not about taking over responsibilities or tasks from the project manager. The clearer the responsibilities of all stakeholders (including your own), the less need for corrective action there will be. The more that all stakeholders are able to predict the effect of an escalation of decision-making to a higher level, the less need for escalations there will be.

Individual contribution

In a hierarchical relationship you can hold someone accountable, but that does not necessarily mean that the person involved *feels responsible*. They might show calculating behaviour, regardless of the effective result, just to avoid being blamed. In the dynamics and complexity of a project, what you need is that people feel responsible and act accordingly, willing to improvise and take initiatives, even when not ordered to. This is called ownership. Examples of project-related ownership discussed in this chapter are risk ownership, benefit ownership and stakeholder relationship ownership.

This ownership should not stand on its own, but be connected to an engagement with the goal of the project: it is a willingness to deliver a specific individual contribution to help achieve this common goal.

Complementary principles

The first and second principles of successful project sponsorship are highly complementary. A shared business case without individual ownership may be an illusion, because 'we are all responsible' may come very close to 'no one feels responsible'. Individual ownership without a shared business case is rigidity and unfocused effort. In the combination of a shared goal and individual ownership lies a powerful creative force.

Stakeholder interaction

Since ownership cannot be imposed upon people, it can only be the result of intensive interaction with stakeholders. This interaction can vary from working together in a steering group to organizing user workshops or meetings focused on participation of large groups of stakeholders (Van der Zouwen, 2011). The essence of this interaction is that people feel heard and respected. This requires you to always be clear about what has already been decided and what is open for discussion.

If you have been transparent about your own position and have allowed stakeholders a fair influence in the process of formulating the business case, you hopefully have created a joint ownership of the business case. If you then call on someone to accept a specific responsibility to achieve this business case, what you are saying to this person equates to 'you are important for all of us', and you may be amazed by the result: many people are happy to be called upon and proud to accept such a responsibility. In this chapter you will read what responsibilities you can assume as a project sponsor and what responsibilities you can delegate to other stakeholders.

The project sponsor: business case owner

As a project sponsor you represent the interests of the sponsoring organization and – on behalf of senior management if applicable – you weigh the benefits against the costs and the risks. Sometimes the project sponsor is called 'the owner of the business case', that is, they are accountable for its realization, which is equivalent to the success of the project. For reasons of clarity and decisiveness in project direction and clear understanding of accountabilities, this role should be fulfilled by no more than one person and they should have an adequate mandate to allow them to manage the realization of the business case (Garland, 2009). In this role you are also responsible for communication with business management and other stakeholders. As a project champion you are permanently in touch with your environment, to check if there are any developments that might influence the business case.

The project sponsor and cost control

Most parties involved in projects have an interest in increasing the scope of the project and/or in raising the quality standards:

- Users and external stakeholders often have an interest in a maximum solution, especially when they don't need to carry the costs themselves.

- Suppliers have an interest in acquiring additional work, at high margins, since they don't need to compete with other suppliers any more.

- For consultants and other specialist staff, schedule overruns lead to extra work hence extra income.

- Specialists in designing roles, such as architects, soon build up a reputation with exclusive (expensive) designs rather than with tight cost control.

- For a project manager, a request for extra functionality or quality is a business routine: while it is the project manager's job to control costs, they will normally welcome any adjustment to schedule and budget increase agreed by the project sponsor.

The only party who can truly countervail all this is the project sponsor, the representative of the line organization, who weighs the costs against the benefits and – even if this is against the interests of all other stakeholders – can reject a change request. This may require courage and this is why weak project sponsorship is practically a guarantee for cost overruns.

The steering group

In order to root stakeholder engagement and to improve the quality of decision-making, you can get yourself surrounded by a steering group with a representation of stakeholders. The steering group of a project serves to align the temporary organization (the project) with the permanent organization (the line organization and its stakeholders). Since you don't want to have everything resting on your shoulders, it is in your interest as a project sponsor that all steering group members actively take up their roles and work well together. In most cases it is not useful to define a long list of responsibilities for each steering group member, so please consider the overview of responsibilities in this chapter as possibilities, and determine for yourself what is useful in a specific situation.

Steering group start-up

A well-functioning steering group does not create itself. At the start of a project, organize a steering group start-up meeting, focused on:

- creating a team spirit;
- creating a shared insight into the business case;
- allowing steering group members to share their worries;
- clarifying individual responsibilities of steering group members;
- agreements about the way to work together.

The participants of such a meeting are the project sponsor, the other members of the steering group and the project manager. Don't invite the whole project team. This will lead to discussions going into too much technical detail, and will create an unsafe environment for steering group members to share their doubts and worries and to openly discuss their responsibilities. Let an independent facilitator lead the session, in order to allow all participants to make a significant contribution.

Steering group: not a democracy

By nature, the project sponsor is the chairperson of the steering group. For important decisions, such as the approval of a plan or a change request, always consult the steering group. But as a project sponsor, you remain accountable for the realization of the business case, which implies that a steering group cannot be a democracy. It is obvious that when all steering group members except for the sponsor want to raise the project budget, the project budget cannot be raised. Furthermore, as a project sponsor you are responsible for the composition of the steering group, including changing it when this improves the project's chances of success.

In order to prevent unjust expectations, be clear about your own accountability for realizing the business case and the limits of the mandate imposed upon you by the organization.

A project sponsor says...

'In our R&D department we are implementing a knowledge management system. In the course of the project the estimates of the amount of hours to completion, instead of decreasing, kept increasing. This was caused again and again by new user requirements, which each time were considered to be very important. As the project sponsor, I started to wonder whether I had invited the right user representatives to the steering group. Recently I stopped looking for consensus and simply turned off the money tab. I now first want them to deliver a working result based on present insights. After that, if anyone has any additional requirements, they can apply for a new project budget.'

Steering group composition

Steering group membership does not come without strings attached. It is not meant just to make decisions that favour the interests of one's own department or one's own grass-roots supporters. Steering group membership comes with responsibilities. As a project sponsor, in order not to carry the burden of the project solely on your shoulders, it is in your interests to assign two main senior management responsibilities to other steering group members, one representing the user interests, called senior user, and one representing the supplier interests, called senior supplier.[1]

Steering group roles

The senior user is the steering group role representing the user interests within the project and accountable for ensuring that user needs are specified correctly, that the solution meets those needs and that it enables the realization of the proposed benefits. This role represents all users in the widest sense of the word, that is, all those who will use, operate, manage, exploit, maintain, sell, buy, rent or inhabit the result of the project.

The senior supplier is the steering group role representing the (internal and external) supplier interests within the project and providing supplier resources, accountable for ensuring compliance of the project result with the baseline (scope, quality, schedule and budget).

If you don't want steering group membership to be a free ride, the concept of working with senior user and senior supplier roles is very powerful.

This chapter assumes that the steering group is fully responsible for all aspects of project direction. In a well-organized company, however, several processes may be in place to take over part of this responsibility. Typically a portfolio manager can take responsibility for the availability of specialist staff, and if the project is part of a programme then the programme manager can take responsibility for user communication and benefit management. Project direction should always be tailored to the context. Before making your own arrangements, check what arrangements have already been made regarding these responsibilities and how they can be coordinated with your project sponsor role.

The project manager: member of the steering group?

The project manager usually participates in steering group meetings. However, they are not a member of the steering group: that would be like an auditor marking their own paper. In addition, their participation might inspire the other steering group members to leave the steering group responsibilities to the project manager instead of taking them themselves ('Surely, we have someone in our midst who is working on the project full time...'). This is a threat to business management commitment and grass-roots support.

The relationship with the project manager is further discussed in detail in Chapter 6.

The senior user

As defined in this chapter, a senior user is accountable for ensuring that the project result will be used in such a way that it will allow the realization of the proposed benefits. By nature, this basic accountability implies a responsibility for ensuring the functional quality of the products. (Do they support business processes? Will they enable us to realize the proposed benefits?) Additionally, a senior user is responsible for ensuring the support amongst users and the availability of users for participation in the creation process, either directly or by drafting specifications and checking products. In case of conflicting user interests, the senior user is responsible for coming to an unambiguous viewpoint on behalf of the users.

Given these responsibilities, the senior user, more than anyone else, has the right to speak out when it comes to defining product requirements. This responsibility of the senior user goes beyond the responsibility of their line function: they are responsible for ensuring the engagement of all users, not only those who belong to their own department. This role can be fulfilled by one or more persons. They will have to consult other user stakeholders on a regular basis.

Before you decide to start a project (or to change it substantially), check if the senior user feels able and is willing to ensure the realization of the proposed benefits with the planned project results, and if they can take care of the necessary availability of users for the creation process. These may be hard questions to answer. But if the answer is 'no' or 'I don't know', you know what you are about to get into and may consider to adjust or withdraw your plans. Or find yourself another senior user.

Tip for agile projects

In agile projects the product owner (also called user representative) represents the user environment and works closely with the development team to set priorities regarding work items to be executed and to decide about functionality. This role comes close to what is defined as the senior user role in this book. See to it that the product owner is not only focused on the definition and the acceptance of work items, but also feels responsible for their implementation and for benefit realization in line with the business case.

The senior supplier

As stated, a senior supplier is accountable for ensuring that the project result is delivered to agreed quality standards and within cost and time agreed and, as such, is responsible for continuity in case the project manager fails or resigns. This implies a responsibility for ensuring the technical quality of the products, the conformity to specifications and the availability of specialist staff. This responsibility goes beyond the responsibility of their line function. They are responsible for all supplier parties involved, not only their own department. They will have to consult other internal and external supplier stakeholders on a regular basis.

Before you decide to start a project (or to change it substantially), check if the senior supplier supports the schedule and the budget and if they have ensured the commitment of other supplier stakeholders.

Tip for the PRINCE2 environment

PRINCE2 provides detailed support to project managers regarding when to create what sort of documentation and what the content should be. Under pressure of time, or by habit, this may lead to standard texts being copied into project documentation without ever coming to life. This may lead to meaningless documentation that is hardly read and is never put into practice. An example of a meaningless, generic role description may look like this:

The senior user will:

- provide the customer's quality expectations and define acceptance criteria for the project;

- ensure that the desired outcome of the project is specified;

- ensure that the project produces products that will deliver the desired outcomes, and meet user requirements. (OGC, 2009)

The above text is taken from a handbook. A more meaningful role description for the same person might look like this:

Mary Johnson, marketing manager, fulfils the role of senior user. She represents our external customers and our Marketing, Sales and Operations departments. Her main challenge will be to ensure that our customers will really want to buy our improved product. She will:

- play a pivotal role towards our customer sounding board and play an active role in social media to keep in touch with our customer's interests and wishes;

- consult the sales manager and the operations manager whenever necessary in order to ensure that she is able to represent their viewpoints in steering group meetings.

A meaningful role description is not generic but specific and can only be developed by involving the person who will fulfil the role.

Link to line management accountabilities

Each steering group role carries specific responsibilities. Allocate these roles in such a way that, as much as possible, they are in line with the line accountabilities of those involved, so that they are fully equipped to make the necessary decisions or to organize them and experience their consequences. A steering group composed in this way allows you to come to a proper trade-off in project decision-making between the business interests (project sponsor), the user requirements (senior user) and the technical aspects (senior supplier). Chapter 5 will look at this in more detail.

Behaviour

In the end, it is not the formal structure that counts, but the behaviour of people. For each of the steering group roles defined, favourable behaviour is:

- **Project sponsor**: as the sponsor of the project, the most important thing is to show that you feel you are the owner of the project and that its success is important to you. The behaviour to support this is to actively share the business case and use it as a foundation for all communication and decision-making (talk the talk, walk the walk). You call on other stakeholders to contribute to project success based on their specific responsibilities, and you pay attention to a good working relationship and open communication with the project manager. You maintain the basic conditions such as the availability of people and other resources, thus creating the circumstances within which the project manager can fulfil their task successfully.

- **Senior user**: the most important thing for a senior user is to show that they feel responsible to ensure that the products will be accepted and used in such a way that this leads to the realization of the proposed benefits. The behaviour to support this is to actively share the business case in the user community; give guidance to the implementation of benefit management and benefit realization; to communicate effectively with the user community in order to ensure that everyone contributes to the specifications wherever necessary; to react quickly when the project manager requests advice regarding user-related subjects such as conflicting requirements; and to intervene directly when people from the user environment are not available according to plan.

- **Senior supplier**: the most important thing for a senior supplier is to show that they feel responsible to ensure that the proposed project result will meet all quality criteria and be delivered on time and to budget. The behaviour to support this is to actively share the business case in the supplier community; communicate effectively with the supplier community in order to ensure that the project gets the right priority; to react quickly when the project manager requests advice regarding supplier-related subjects such as technical requirements and standards; and to intervene directly when specialists or other supplier resources are not available according to plan.

Teamwork

The foundation of a successful steering group is a joint commitment to the success of the project. It is essential that all steering group members support the business case, communicate openly, call on each other for each one's role and work together in a constructive way. This is about showing leadership, taking responsibility and teamwork, inside and outside the steering group meetings. The fact that each member has their own responsibility should not lead to individualism and a culture of passing the buck.

A project sponsor says...

'In our organization managers used to participate in steering groups to defend their departments' interests against possible negative effects of a project. A steering group member had rights without duties and a steering group meeting sometimes was a round of shooting the project manager, no strings attached. What we demand now – that steering group members accept a share of responsibility for the success of the project – implies an enormous shift of culture.'

The steering group: small is beautiful

One of the pitfalls of working with steering groups is making them too large, driven by stakeholder groups who all want to be represented directly. This can hamper efficient decision-making and mean that none of the members feel personally responsible for the project. Therefore, don't make a steering group larger than absolutely necessary. Stakeholders can influence the project result by other means: see Chapter 3 about the third principle, *focus on deliverables*.

Appointing one person in each of the three roles can be seen as a practical standard. In the case of a simple project – for instance affecting only one department, and the head of the department is the project sponsor – one person could combine several roles. An obvious choice in that case is to combine the role of project sponsor and senior user. Complex project environments might require that a role is shared by several people. But if more than one member of a steering group has a similar role, see to it that each one has an individual responsibility, for instance related to specific stakeholder groups.

Individual responsibilities

Several specific responsibilities can be assigned to steering group members:

- the responsibility for ensuring stakeholder engagement;
- the responsibility to ensure benefit realization;
- the responsibility for specific risks;
- the responsibility for assurance.

Who is responsible for ensuring stakeholder engagement?

In practice, the project manager will frequently communicate with stakeholders at an operational level. The steering group members, however, remain responsible for the boundaries of this communication and for staying in touch with their own grass roots. There are two important reasons for this. One is that the visible support of line managers for the business case contributes to the credibility of, and support for, the project. The other is that, in order to prevent any unnecessary resistance, information that could be regarded as 'sensitive' is best transferred by a representative of line management. Line management is represented in the steering group and is responsible to oversee the total need for communication and to determine which communication should take place through the line, and what communication can be left to the project manager.

In the steering group, pay attention to creating a common understanding of the business case as a basis for communication with stakeholders outside the steering group, and see to it that all communication by steering group members is consistent with the business case. Agreements to all communication can be registered in a communication plan.

A steering group can only function well, if it retains good relationships with all stakeholders, inside as well as outside one's own organization. Therefore, see to it that each steering group member knows which stakeholders to maintain contact with. Vice versa it is important that each stakeholder knows who takes part in the steering group on behalf of them ('my representative in the steering group'), so that they can call on this person when necessary.

In a steering group meeting, discuss who are to be considered as stakeholders, and for each stakeholder which steering group member is responsible for ensuring their engagement: the stakeholder relationship owner. You can support this discussion and record the result with a stakeholder relationship matrix (see Table 2.1).

TABLE 2.1   Stakeholder relationship matrix

Stakeholder	Stakeholder relationship owner			
	Heather (project sponsor)	Najib (senior user)	Mary (senior user)	Peter (senior supplier)
Board of directors	X			
Division directors	X			
Works council	X			
Customer council		X		
Customers		X		
Account managers		X		
Information managers			X	
Regional management			X	
Employees, department X		X		
Employees, department Y			X	
Finance and accounting			X	
ICT department				X
External ICT supplier				X
Media	X			

Who is responsible for ensuring benefit realization?

A business case often mentions 'expected benefits'. These are of no value, however, as it is all about realized benefits. Expected benefits without specific commitments to realize them are a breeding ground for overestimating benefits, and hence for a too rosy picture of the business case, with too optimistic decision-making as a result.

Benefit management aims to effectively realize the proposed benefits of change. This requires the following responsibilities:

- The project sponsor is accountable for the success of the project and sees to it that others involved adequately pick up their roles.

- The senior user is responsible for ensuring that the relevant stakeholders are adequately engaged in the process of benefit management, in order to allow them to connect with the goal of the project, and are willing to take responsibility as benefit owners (responsible for the realization of benefits). In a simple project, the project sponsor can fulfil the role of senior user themselves.

- The benefit owners are the ones who take responsibility to realize one or more specific benefits. Often, the senior user is also the owner of part of the benefits. In a simple project, the senior user can be the only benefit owner.

For effective benefit management, it is essential that benefit ownership is not (only) a formal accountability, but that a benefit owner *feels* connected with the goal of the project – realizing its business case – and effectively *feels* responsible to contribute to this by means of certain benefits (achievements).[2] Mostly it is necessary to hold one or more workshops with stakeholders to map the required benefits, what they depend on and who takes responsibility to realize them. Such workshops can lead to the insight that certain benefits are not realistic or that additional investments are needed before certain benefits can be realized. In these cases, adjusting the business case can be necessary in order to maintain the commitment. That is why, as a project sponsor, you cannot simply leave benefit management to the senior user. For a more detailed discussion on benefit management please refer to Chapter 7.

Who is responsible for specific risks?

A risk is something that might happen in the future that will impact on the success of the project. A risk owner is someone who has taken responsibility to keep an eye on a specific risk and to undertake necessary actions as soon as possible when a risk effectively occurs. Therefore, when assigning risk ownership, the basic principle is 'all hands on deck'. This means that the person who is best able to directly notice the occurrence of a specific risk should accept the risk ownership, regardless of their role in the project organization. When a steering group member is in a better position to notice the occurrence of a certain risk than the project manager, then it makes sense to assign the risk ownership to this steering group member and not to delegate it to the project manager.

More information about dealing with risk can be found in Chapter 9.

Who is responsible for project assurance?

The fact that steering group members carry responsibility for a project implies that they should supervise the project or have the project supervised on their behalf. When things go wrong, 'I didn't know that' or 'the project manager hadn't told me' are not valid excuses.

What is assurance?

Assurance is a safeguard. When something goes wrong, there is a provision that ensures things will turn out right anyway. For example, a mountaineer is secured by means of a rope: when their hands and feet (primary system) slip off the mountain wall, they are still hanging on a rope (secondary system). After some corrective actions, control can be handed back to the primary system. The mountaineer hasn't fallen and can continue climbing. Of course there is no such thing as a 100 per cent guarantee, not in mountaineering and not in project management.

A manager in the construction industry said: 'Project assurance? We simply call this a supervisor, someone who walks around the construction site on behalf of the customer.'

Independent supervision on the realization of a project by or on behalf of a steering group member is called project assurance. When you, as a steering group member, delegate part of your assurance role, be clear about what should be assured and about the framework for assurance.

Project assurance is not necessarily limited to a supervising role. When useful, persons in a project assurance role can also advise the project manager, as long as this does not endanger their independency with respect to the project manager.

Delegate selectively

Often it is better for steering group members to delegate part of their assurance role, because otherwise it gets insufficient attention by pressure of their operational duties. Often, a check by an independent specialist with the right competences is more effective and cheaper than a check by a steering group member during a meeting. However, the responsibility remains with the members of the steering group and too much control is over the top. Therefore, be selective when assigning project assurance roles: focus on those aspects that are vital for realization of the business case. Discuss this with the persons who are to execute the assurance activities, so that they can see their own role in the perspective of the goal of the project. See to it that each person taking on a delegated project assurance role knows on behalf of which steering group member they fulfil this role, that is, which steering group member they will report to. When it is not clear on whose behalf the assurance activities take place, they might become a purpose on their own, with obsolete control activities and bureaucracy as a result. In Chapter 5 you will find more information about project assurance and how to organize this effectively.

Other responsibilities

In addition to the responsibilities described above, the steering group is also responsible for ensuring the management of scope, quality, planning and cost, and decision-making on changes to these. This is discussed in Chapter 3 about the third principle, *focus on deliverables*, and in Chapter 4 on the fourth principle, *empower the project manager*.

Appendix 4 summarizes all responsibilities and accountabilities relating to the direction and management of a project.

Summary

The second principle, *organize ownership*, helps you to get stakeholders to accept specific individual responsibilities in connection with the business case. It contributes to:

- More effectivity: when business managers assume individual responsibility, this contributes to stakeholder engagement, benefit management, cost management, risk management and quality management.

- More efficient meetings: because steering group members also have clear responsibilities outside the meetings, the steering group meetings do not need to cover all the details.

- Efficiency and agility in project realization: when the project manager cannot solve an issue themselves, they always know which steering group member is responsible, so that they can address this steering group member instead of escalating the issue to the whole steering group.

- More reliable information and less risk that the project manager keeps issues hidden: because steering group members get independent information through their assurance roles, the information provision of the steering group does not depend on the project manager alone.

- Your own ownership of the business case is the basis to countervail the pressure of other stakeholders to unnecessarily increase the scope or raise the quality standards.

- Maybe the most essential thing: more support for the project. By assigning clear responsibilities, for example as steering group member, risk owner or benefit owner, the participation of stakeholders is strings attached – and as a project sponsor you don't carry the weight of the project on your shoulders alone. This will save you a lot of time.

Notes

1 In this book I prefer the terms 'senior user' and 'senior supplier' for these steering group roles instead of 'user representative' and 'supplier representative' in order to avoid confusion with other user/supplier representatives outside the steering group. In real life, in the context of a steering group, if everyone knows what you mean there is no reason why you shouldn't simply use a term such as user representative, customer representative or tenants' representative.

2 For an inspiring view on performance management and the risks of formal accountabilities to achieve this, read *Transforming Performance Measurement* (Spitzer, 2007).

The third principle: focus on deliverables

03

FIGURE 3.1 The third principle

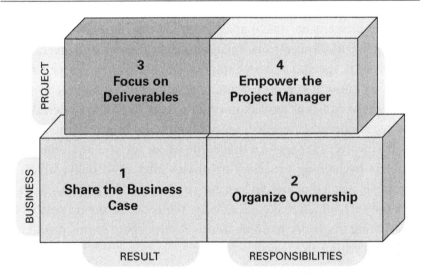

Go for the result

Projects usually are divided into phases, processes and activities: things people do. As a project sponsor, however, when you assess a project plan your first concern is not what people are going to *do*, but the result, the *output*: what you are going to get, when you are going to get it and what it is going to cost. Users, too, are primarily interested in the tangible results of a project. Also when dealing with suppliers, the focus should be on what tangible results they deliver. It is the resulting deliverable that gives activities a meaning and makes them concrete. That is why in a good, transparent plan, deliverables (end deliverables as well as intermediate deliverables) are the main focus of attention.[1]

Deliverable

A deliverable is any unique and verifiable product, result or capability to perform a service that must be produced to complete the process, phase or project.

Scope management, time management, cost management and quality management all need to be related to the same set of deliverables in order to be specific and meaningful. During realization you always want to know if the project manager is going to make it to realize these deliverables as agreed, in order to enable you to undertake corrective action when needed. Indeed, you want to go for the result.

The project manager can make life easier for you and other stakeholders by naming processes or phases after their deliverables. For example, instead of 'design' (an activity) it could be 'approved design' (an output), which makes clear what the result of the process is, that everything necessary to come to this result is part of this process and that everything else is not.

Clear scope

A clear scope is based on an agreement about the deliverables to be realized, which means that:

- the users are willing to use, manage and maintain these deliverables with the defined quality in such a way that this leads to the proposed benefits;

- the internal and/or external supplier(s) are able to realize these deliverables within the conditions defined;

- the project sponsor is willing to invest in these deliverables, because they are convinced that they will allow them to realize the business case.

Experience shows that the question of which tangible result a project should exactly deliver can lead to a lot of discussion. This discussion is useful because in the end you cannot avoid it anyway and, the later the right answers are found, the higher the cost will be for corrective action. Not all deliverables need to be specified in detail instantly: in a proper project plan the deliverables are, by and large, defined in more detail during the course of the project.

Deliverables and commitments

If you discuss a plan for approval in the steering group, call on people based on their specific responsibility. When discussing a list of deliverables, ask the senior user if they approve them, if they have had their specifications checked by the right people, and if they are convinced that with these deliverables the users will be able to realize the proposed benefits. When discussing the schedule and budget, ask the senior supplier if they have had them checked by the right people and if they can ensure the availability of the right specialists to realize these deliverables. When discussing the definition of intermediate quality control activities and final acceptance of the deliverables by the users, ask the senior user if they can ensure the availability of the right people from the user side. Without this foundation – the commitment of users and suppliers to the deliverables to be realized and to the availability of the resources required – there is a good chance that later on this will lead to unnecessary extra cost and delays, or total stagnation.

Examples of deliverables

A deliverable can simply be of material nature, such as a site ready for building or an approved document. What counts is that there is a result that can be checked and proven. Sometimes it is about people who should have a certain knowledge or capacity after the project. An example of such a deliverable is informed inhabitants. You can define what sort of information the inhabitants should have and you could check if they are indeed informed. Another example is trained employees. You can define what capability these employees should have and check if they indeed have it.

Ambiguous deliverables

Some terms used to define deliverables are ambiguous. A classic example of this is the term 'process', for instance in 'a new business process for dealing with complaints'. There is quite a difference between (in order of increasing scope):

- a description of a defined business process developed by the project team;
- a description of a business process accepted by stakeholders;
- a business process proven in a pilot;
- an implemented business process.

In the first case the result is a document without a formal status, in the last case something has changed in the real world, a challenge that might be endlessly bigger. It might take a week for a project team to define a new logistic process, but it might take a year to develop and implement it. Therefore, in order to manage expectations it is often necessary to use additions such as 'accepted' or 'implemented'.

Projects with an unclear end deliverable

With some projects it is even harder than with others to define the end deliverable at the beginning. Take for instance research projects, projects in which stakeholders step-by-step seek for a solution, or projects in which it is not certain at the start that the solution is feasible. Even in these cases, deliverable-oriented questions will help to clarify the scope:

- As a result of a research project, do you expect a report? Or do you expect a prototype of a solution?

- As a result of a project in which stakeholders step-by-step seek for a solution, do you expect a definition of the solution? Or an implemented solution?

- As a result of a project of which the feasibility of the solution is not certain, do you expect a report of the feasibility study, or do you expect more?

The same goes for the intermediate results in these kinds of projects: have them defined as deliverables. Even when the total project costs are still highly uncertain, this enables you to determine what you are willing to invest in a first intermediate deliverable.

Tip for agile projects

In agile projects, the principle *focus on deliverables* presented in this book should refer to the product backlog (or project backlog): the list of work items in order of priority to be realized by the development team. As a project sponsor you remain accountable for getting value for money, so also if you don't perform the product owner role yourself be aware of what work items you are investing in, what purpose they serve and how they are prioritized.

Ghost deliverables

Some project managers are eager to present results as deliverables, and they even list deliverables that they can never create. Some real-life examples include:

- support in the production environment;
- a decision of the board of directors on our new policy;
- a 4 per cent reduction of the average call time in our call centre.

The question is: can a project manager create these kinds of results as deliverables within schedule and budget, in order for line management to use them? The answer is obviously no, only line management themselves can realize these results. If you allow these kinds of results to be included in a project plan disguised as deliverables, you could actually allow the steering group to be misled: it might lead them to think that the project manager will take care of all this. Beware of these 'ghost deliverables' and only allow deliverables to be included of which the project manager can reasonably manage their creation. When things like creating support, achieving board decisions or realizing benefits are at stake, see to it that a steering group member takes responsibility.

Ensure that the project manager has a concrete and realistic task that is the realization of a number of deliverables for which they can be held to account. What kind of deliverables a project manager can effectively realize depends on the circumstances, such as the expected resistance to change as opposed to spontaneous cooperation of stakeholders. In one project it may be possible to have a project manager deliver an 'accepted solution' or even an 'implemented new business process' on time and to budget, while in yet another project this might not be realistic.

Users are interested in deliverables, not in projects

Users often are hardly interested in 'what is going to happen': this is largely of a specialist nature and irrelevant to non-specialists. On the other hand, most users see the results of a project (the end deliverable or deliverables) as very interesting. Most likely they will have an opinion on what they are going to get (or would like to get) and will be willing to share it. Therefore, deliverables are the essence of scope management.

A project can engage users in the specification of deliverables, the assessment of intermediate deliverables and the acceptance of the end deliverable, or in creating deliverables together with specialists, thus reducing the need for formal specification and control. A focus on deliverables is a prerequisite for user engagement.

A project sponsor says...

In the steering committee of a logistics project, several user groups were represented each by their own steering group member:

> 'Because the project was to impact the whole chain, they found it hard to imagine what exactly was going to change. As a consequence they didn't feel engaged. Until one of them asked: "But what exactly is it that we are going to get?" The project manager made a list of the concrete deliverables that he intended to realize. This instantly triggered a discussion. People now started to get the picture. Remarks went from "that will never work" to "but if that's what we want, then why don't we just…" The meeting led to some improvements of the plan, which I'm sure prevented later implementation problems, and to more support for the plan amongst users.'

Ensuring quality

Ensuring functional quality – that is, the extent to which the deliverables effectively support the business processes – is a senior user accountability. Ensuring technical quality – that is, the extent to which the deliverables comply with specifications, are reliable and comply with relevant standards – is a senior supplier accountability. But how can steering group members carry these responsibilities without having to check all details themselves? Again, a deliverable-oriented approach can help, whether a deliverable is being developed in a classical way (specify, design, build, test, accept) or in an iterative way (step-by-step a team of users and specialists create a better version of a deliverable, especially in the ICT world). In both cases, the same questions are relevant: what is it that we are going to get, who is allowed to determine when it is good enough, and within which framework? By having these matters clearly defined, a steering group member can control quality, without checking these deliverables themselves. Deliverables are at the essence of quality management.

> ### Tip for agile projects
>
> In agile projects, testers often have a far-reaching mandate to sign off products. According to various authors (for example, Kniberg, 2007) it is up to the tester to make sure that the intentions of the product owner (the person who is responsible for deploying the product, a role comparable to the senior user role) are understood by the team. From a business perspective I would emphasize the reverse: it is up to the product owner to ensure that their intentions are understood by the tester and the team.

By seeing to it that the right user representatives check and accept the right intermediate deliverables (such as 'requirements document', 'design' or 'prototype'), the senior user can make sure that the users are appropriately engaged with the project. Any quality issues will surface sooner, allowing timely corrective action to be taken in order to secure the required end deliverable. This pays back by means of more support amongst users; fewer implementation problems; fewer complaints after transfer of the deliverables to the operational and maintenance environment; and less rework. See Chapter 8 for more details about how to achieve quality without having to check the deliverables yourself.

Getting a grip on progress

The criterion for progress measurement can now be clearly defined: the yardstick for progress measurement will be the actual completion dates of (intermediate) deliverables completed as compared to their planned completion dates (or phases/processes if they are unambiguously focused on the realization of a specific deliverable). By defining 'completed' as 'approved by reviewers appointed by the steering group', progress measurement is objectified, or at least independent from the project manager. For the project manager, this makes it hard to – consciously or subconsciously – cover up stagnation or to draw a too rosy picture of project progress. By focusing project control on completion dates of deliverables (instead of completion dates of activities or phases), you will have a more objective insight into project status, and setbacks will be brought to light as early as possible. The status of deliverables is the foundation of reliable time management.

Getting a grip on cost

Just like quality management and time management, cost management should be linked to the status of tangible results: deliverables (or phases/processes if they are unambiguously focused on the realization of a specific deliverable). A good project budget should list the expected costs of each of the intermediate deliverables to be realized (at an appropriate aggregation level). A good performance report should compare this to the real costs of the deliverables realized so far. During project realization, each time an intermediate deliverable is realized this provides an objective foundation for financial status reporting, independent of subjective estimates. In short, a focus on deliverables is the foundation of effective cost management.

Of course, for work in progress (deliverables started but not yet completed) you will still need to rely on subjective estimates of specialists ('We expect to need £10,000 more in order to complete deliverable X'). But a good plan is decomposed in such a way that, at each moment in time, most deliverables are either completed or not yet started. This way, only a limited part of your budget control will depend on subjective estimates of work in progress, which provides you with a more reliable picture of the financial status of the project and helps you to get cost overruns to the surface as soon as possible.

An additional advantage of a budget in which the items are clearly related to deliverables is that for you as a sponsor it brings more transparency to what you get for your money, which makes it easier to think about possible cost reductions.

Consistency

In short, a good plan is a transparent plan and hence a plan based on clarity of the deliverables to be realized. All relevant sections of the plan – on scope, requirements, quality, schedule and budget – refer to the same collection of deliverables. If you compare the sections of the plan, it is easy to see for each deliverable what the requirements are, what the expected quality is, when it will be completed and what it will cost. This way, it is easy to check consistency and completeness of a new or changed plan (for instance: 'Has everything been planned that has been specified?' or 'Has everything been budgeted that has been planned?'). This is not only beneficial for the project sponsor, but also for the project manager. A clear insight into deliverables makes it easier to analyse the impact of changes and helps to define the scope of activities to be delegated. For a more detailed discussion on plans and performance reports please refer to Chapter 10.

Tip for the PRINCE2 environment

In PRINCE2 training courses, project managers are taught to draw product breakdown structures (PBS, a decomposition of the end product into subproducts) and product flow diagrams (PFD, a visual presentation of the order of creation of products). Sometimes there is more focus on learning these techniques than on their application and purpose. As a consequence you might encounter a plan with a correct PBS and PFD, but with a schedule and budget that are not based on them. The purpose of a PBS is to create consistency throughout the plan. The budget, the schedule and other relevant sections of the plan should indeed be based on it.

Summary

The third principle, *focus on deliverables*, is the ideal foundation for effectively directing the project manager to deliver the required project result. It provides a lot of benefits:

- more clarity about scope;
- clearer expectations;
- lower cost, because conflicting expectations come to the surface sooner (the later these expectations come to the surface, the more expensive);

- more stakeholder support through more transparency;
- a grip on quality without having to check the deliverables yourself;
- more transparent and reliable reporting, hence less last-minute surprises and more time for corrective actions;
- fewer cost overruns and fewer schedule overruns, because a clear scope helps not to waste energy on matters that are outside scope;
- less rework.

The time you allow to be spent on defining the deliverables to be realized and confirming stakeholder support for them will pay back many times.

Note

1 These are the so-called business deliverables, which are the deliverables that the organization actually needs to perform its operations, as opposed to management deliverables, which are plans and reports and the like, the necessary overhead to manage a project. In this book the term 'deliverables' refers to business deliverables, unless stated otherwise.

04

The fourth principle: empower the project manager

FIGURE 4.1 The fourth principle

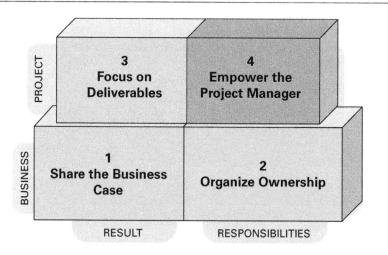

Balanced relationship

A balanced relationship between responsibilities and authorities is a prerequisite for an employee to adequately influence their achievements. It is a condition for motivation and effectivity and disturbance of this balance leads to stress and malfunctioning. Thus, one of the challenges of successful project sponsorship is to create a realistic distribution of responsibilities and authorities between yourself and the project manager. This requires the willingness to give the project manager well-defined responsibilities and to sufficiently empower them to achieve them: a clear mandate, including room for decision-making. This is the basis for an appropriate monitoring and control mechanism.

The project manager's responsibilities

The primary responsibility of the project manager is the delivery of the *results* as agreed, in conformity to *requirements* and within certain *conditions*:

- The *results*, in order to be concrete, should be defined as deliverables: see Chapter 3 about the third principle, *focus on deliverables*.
- The *requirements* of these results mainly refer to their specifications, quality, timeliness and cost.
- The *conditions* for the project manager to deliver the results are, for example, the correctness of specifications and the non-occurrence of certain calamities, but also the availability of budget and employees, and timely decision-making by the project sponsor.

The fourth principle, *empower the project manager*, is closely related to the third principle, *focus on deliverables*. When the deliverables to be realized are not clear, it is very hard to define a concrete responsibility for the project manager.

Tip for agile projects

Agile project teams are to a large extent self-organizing and the team members are supposed to take responsibility for their own work, picking work items from the top of the product backlog. In the ideal situation, the classical project manager as someone who tells people what to do has become superfluous. Large agile projects, however, do need a project manager in a facilitating and organizing role. Their responsibilities are, among others (Hoogendoorn, 2014):

- to make a project plan, covering the agreements between the sponsor and the team, the acceptance criteria and how to deal with the iterations;

- risk management, which in an agile environment implies that the team preferably realizes the high-risk items in the first iterations;

- to manage expectations of the sponsor and other stakeholders;

- to organize the kick offs and evaluations of the iterations, including their facilities;

- to lay down the result of an iteration kick-off meeting in an iteration plan (often not more than one page or a spreadsheet);

- to monitor progress;

- to externally represent the team to the project sponsor and the steering group.

Commitment

Every project sponsor expects the project manager to be committed to the success of the project (as defined in the Introduction of this book). The actual responsibility of the project manager, however, can only lie in the realization of the agreed deliverables, including their handover and/or implementation and the proper support of steering group decision-making. If you want a project manager to be effectively committed, then be prepared to negotiate the conditions. When the project manager deems themselves able to deliver the required results within the proposed conditions and accepts their assignment, there is an agreement between project sponsor and project manager. Maintain the agreed conditions in order to maintain the project manager's commitment.

A project sponsor says...

'Mostly it is easy to recognize a novice project manager: they don't give their own assessment of the feasibility, do not question the conditions and do not demand authorities.'

Management stages

Empowering the project manager is very much in your own interest as a project sponsor. Defining the right mandate will help you to be involved and give strategic direction when needed and let the project manager make decisions when possible, thus saving you time. Without an explicit mandate for your project manager you cannot account for the success of the project.

Unfortunately, it is seldom possible to delegate the project to the project manager as a whole. The defined end deliverable is often not clear enough, the environment is too dynamic and there is growing insight. These are all reasons why you have to stay involved for intermediate decision-making. The most feasible way to still give the project manager a clear mandate is to divide the project into parts that can be demarcated clearly enough to be delegated, so-called management stages.[1] The size of these management stages depends on what you can reasonably oversee: one stage may be longer than another. For each management stage the project manager is given a budget and the authorities needed to realize it.

Management by exception

In some situations you want to be advised as soon as possible in order to be able to intervene directly when needed. Therefore, it is also necessary to determine beyond which limits the project manager must alarm you right away: tolerances or 'alarm limits'. The management stage in combination with the agreed stage tolerances can be seen as 'the length and the width' of the project manager's mandate.

This is called management by exception: it allows the project manager to function independently when possible and to ring the alarm directly in the case of an exception – that is, when the tolerances are forecast to be exceeded. Thus, on the one hand, the project manager and his team have room to work in a motivated way and, on the other, as a project sponsor with your steering group you will be involved in a timely way in making decisions whenever needed:

- at the end of a management stage in order to give the project manager a mandate for the next stage;

- in case of exceptions during the execution of a management stage in order to take corrective action, that is to change or revoke this mandate.

Of course, you can always take the initiative yourself to convene the steering group, triggered by developments in the project environment. The steering group does not always have to meet physically, the decision can also be made in a conference call or by the chair, the project sponsor, after consultation of the members of the steering group.

A project sponsor says...

'In an attempt to maintain tight control, we hadn't given the project manager any explicit mandate. But the schedule was slipping right from the beginning of the project. In fact we had very little control. We never consciously made the decision to continue, change the plan or to stop.'

Stage plan

In order to keep the steering group from sinking into details it is important to make a clear distinction between the responsibility of the steering group (strategic direction) and that of the project manager (daily management). Therefore, the project manager should be explicitly empowered for each management stage. Indeed, only with an explicit mandate can it be made clear as to what issues the project manager is allowed to deal with themselves, and when they have to escalate to the steering group. A clear mandate defines the deliverables to be realized, who is competent to check their quality, their cost, the schedule to realize them and the tolerances (alarm limits) already mentioned. This mandate refers to a management stage and is therefore called a stage plan. Such a stage plan is not meant to set the realization in stone, but as a baseline for performance measurement and reporting, in order to enable proper and timely corrective action. Of course, it is the project manager who drafts the stage plan to be approved by the steering group.

Reporting

Within the framework of a stage plan with tolerances the project manager can permanently assess the feasibility of the present stage to be completed within the agreed limits. As long as they expect that this is the case, they can account retrospectively in periodic reports, for instance at the end of each month. This is called *performance reporting*, progress reporting or highlight reporting. As soon as they expect that they will exceed their tolerances – that is, the limits of their mandate – they should not await the end of the reporting period but raise the alarm directly. This is called *exception reporting*.

Performance reporting

In a performance report the project manager looks back on the past reporting period and looks forward to the coming period. They compare their expectations regarding the end of the current management stage with the stage plan. By showing that the deviations are within tolerance, they underpin that project realization is under control. There is no need for decision-making and no need for the steering group to hold a formal meeting. Of course all other kinds of contact can be desirable, and the steering group remains responsible for ensuring the reliability of the performance reports.

Exception reporting

The first thing that counts in an exception report is speed. As a project sponsor you will want to know right away when the project is out of control. In most environments it is obvious that the first contact about an exception should be face to face. You can thus discuss directly with the project manager how to continue. A good project manager understands your business case and, based on this, will advise you. The main options are to stop or to continue, and the latter may entail changes to scope, quality requirements, budget or schedule. You can also intervene in the governance and management of the project, for instance by changing the composition or responsibilities of the steering group, or by replacing the project manager. When you order the adjustment of the stage plan, and possibly the project plan, and the steering group has approved this new plan (also called exception plan), then the baseline of the project has been changed. This means that from that moment on the project manager has to account based on this new version of the plan.

Tip for the PRINCE2 environment

It is a popular misunderstanding that PRINCE2 prescribes the use of all kinds of documents. The method defines information flows at a functional level, leaving it open as to how this information is to be organized and transferred. In many environments there are no reasons why an exception report could not be transferred orally, especially when it is followed by an exception plan (adapted plan) that records the changes to the baseline. In many situations there is also no reason why an exception plan could not simply consist of the original plan plus an attachment with the approved change request.

If during a reporting period no exceptions have been reported, then the performance report at the end of the reporting period should underpin that project execution is under control – that is, within tolerances.

'Where I work now there is little experience with exception reporting, so I only get periodical performance reports. But still then I want to know what their purpose is. The key question is: is it a report to inform me that the project is under control? Or does the project manager want me to take action? They must be clear about this. And apart from any formal reporting arrangements, I make it perfectly clear in which cases they have to alarm me immediately.'

Fewer meetings?

Assigning a clear responsibility to the project manager, by means of stage plans, in principle enables the steering group to meet less often – that is, only when decisions have to be made. However, it is not advisable to stop meeting periodically right away and only meet at stage transitions or when the project manager reports an exception, as this would most likely result in the steering group not maintaining control. In most cases, a number of steps should be taken first to improve governance and control, and thus create the conditions for management by exception:

- the division of the project into management stages;
- a clear focus of each management stage on the realization of deliverables;
- the definition of tolerances for each management stage;
- the establishment of a clear reporting mechanism;
- tailor-made project assurance;
- a clear focus of the steering group meeting-agenda on decision-making, which includes a proper and timely preparation of meetings with decisions to be made.

Even when the conditions for management by exception are there, some managers still prefer regular steering group meetings. In the words of a manager in the insurance industry:

> 'For large projects we hold short weekly steering group meetings. This way we stay together closely, help each other and can discuss possible misunderstandings.'

In case you make this choice, the main points of attention are: the focus on the business case (instead of sinking into the details of realization), assigning individual responsibilities to steering group members (instead of only 'we will work it out together'), clarity about the project result to be delivered and a clear empowerment of the project manager.

In some organizations the influence of agile can be felt in the functioning of steering groups, striving to meet more often but for shorter time (sometimes in stand-up meetings like an agile project team, to make sure that people don't talk too long), and relying on direct short-term feedback rather than extensive documentation. However, for steering group members who want to consult their grass roots before making a decision, a meeting formally prepared with proposed decisions might be preferable.

Check the business case

In the case of changes or exceptions, when you make a decision as to if or how you want to continue the project, you check – sometimes on the spot, sometimes after thorough investigation – if the business case of the project is still valid. 'Valid' means that the business case still supports the strategic goals of the organization. This way, you maintain the strategic focus and keep the project from taking on a life of its own, even in the case of changing circumstances and growing insight.

Motivator

The division of the project into management stages not only helps the steering group to control the project, it is also a motivator for the project team. Indeed, in addition to the faraway end goal of the project, this provides a concrete objective nearby that must be achieved: the timely completion of the management stage to support steering group decision-making.

Which management stages?

How to divide the project into management stages depends on the nature of the project. One project requires more strategic checkpoints than another, one project lasts longer or is more complex than another, and you can give one project manager more responsibility and authorities than another. Sometimes the nature of the project requires specific stages, such as 'supplier selection', 'building and reviewing a model' or 'proof of concept'.

The best division into management stages is found in cooperation with the project manager and based on a trade-off of strategic and practical considerations. Too many management stages means

Tip for agile projects

Agile projects are divided into short stages, called iterations or sprints, with a fixed length, for instance two or four weeks. In each iteration the development team tries to realize a number of work items, selected from the product backlog at the beginning of the iteration. Direct feedback is ensured by the close contact between users and specialists and the short duration of the iterations, allowing you frequently to reprioritize and to decide on project continuation. In most cases this makes formal tolerances superfluous, but beware of scope creep.

unnecessary overhead because of too much formal decision-making, whereas too few management stages means an unrealistically large mandate for the project manager, a lack of strategic control and thus a lack of business ownership.

The minimum number of management stages

There is one stage that we almost always need. This has to do with the fact that the project is an investment, and that we are used to making investment decisions in two steps. For instance, when you want to renovate your house, your *first decision* is that you are going to spend time investigating what the possibilities are and what it will cost, probably working on this together with an architect or a contractor. When you have a design and a cost estimate, you make the *second decision*, that is to actually invest. This first stage, between the basic decision to start a project and the decision to actually invest, is the planning stage (also called definition stage or initiation stage). At this stage, the project manager is responsible for underpinning the investment decision to be made. The level of detail needed to complete this stage will be different for each project. In the example of the renovation, one houseowner might want to know what it will cost to adjust the furnishings and the garden, whereas another might

---

Tip for agile projects

An agile project does not consist of iterations only. Before the first iteration can start, there needs to be agreements between the sponsor and the development team about the project goal, the budget, the roles and responsibilities, the deadlines, the way of working and acceptance criteria. This does not mean that an agile project should start with a waterfall approach. Instead of preparing a detailed plan and then trying to get it approved by the project sponsor, the project manager can also choose a more agile approach, seeking permanent interaction with stakeholders and short feedback loops with the project sponsor. Thus a joint plan is created, of which the final approval is just a formality.

not need this information in order to make the same decision. The minimum number of management stages (that would suffice for a simple project) is two: the planning stage just mentioned and a realization stage to deliver the result.

The total amount of information you need as a project sponsor to make the investment decision at the end of the planning stage is called the project management plan (also called project initiation documentation, PID). In addition to a description of the business case, this contains the baselines for managing scope, cost, time and quality, and it can contain the approaches to communication, stakeholder management, risk management, change management, configuration management, procurement and human resource management. It is a common pitfall to keep working on a project management plan endlessly (there is always room for improvement), thus spending more and more money without making a formal investment decision. Be clear about what information you need to be able to make the basic investment decision and let the project manager focus on this, thus allowing you to make the investment decision before having spent too much.

Courage

'In our organization the dominant culture is: think positive, believe in success and go for it. If you want to do a risk assessment, you can quite easily be seen as a universal complainer, as someone who is not really willing. In our company it takes courage to claim enough time for project preparation.'

The planning stage is followed by one or more realization stages. In order to remain in control, and not to be taken for granted by the project manager, it is advisable to make a concise and explicit go/no-go decision for each management stage, in consultation with the steering group when applicable. Avoid detailed discussions about the deliverables realized so far: when the decision about continuation to the next stage is about to be made, the deliverables should already have been checked by reviewers, appointed under the responsibility of the steering group (if necessary, the decision on the formal release of these deliverables can be made by the steering group). The discussion in the steering group should mainly focus on the project status relative to the business case and the risks, what can be learned from the past stage and whether and how to continue the project.

Communication opportunity

Use the transition to a next stage as a communication opportunity, thereby, of course, referring to the business case. For grass-roots support of the project it is beneficial that management (represented in the steering group) shows that it is still behind the project.

Summary

The fourth principle, *empower the project manager*, creates optimum conditions for the project manager to manage their team and work together with the steering group. It offers the following advantages:

- It saves you time, because it prevents unnecessary consultation caused by unclear responsibilities and authorities.

- Because the steering group does not sink into details but remains focused on strategic control and direction, you ensure the business focus of project direction.

- It is motivating for the project manager and their team, because they have a clear framework for decision-making, which enables them to make a clearly recognizable contribution to the success of the project.

- Assigning a budget and agreeing on tolerances per stage combines explicit room for the project manager and their team with full responsibility of the steering group. By choosing the right restrictions you create an effective combination of motivation, flexibility and control.

- Holding fewer steering group meetings and focusing them on decision-making furthers the efficiency of project direction.

Supervision of project realization does not take place during steering group meetings but outside these meetings, based on performance reporting and project assurance, and, when needed, through informal contact that the steering group members have with the project manager.

Chapter 6 will discuss the relationship with the project manager in detail.

Note

1 A management stage is not always the same as a technical phase. Technical phases such as design or realization are defined from the viewpoint of the creation process. But in projects often one deliverable is already being realized, while another still has to be designed, and yet another is already handed over to the operational environment, so technical phases can overlap. Management stages refer to all activities that have to be done during a certain period of time. So that management stages do not overlap, the next management stage only begins after the completion of the previous one.

Summary of Part 1

The four principles of successful project sponsorship are:

- *Share the business case*. Advantages: a continued focus on the intended business results; more support for the project; less room for conflicts of interests between stakeholders; and better decision-making on details based on a motivated trade-off between user and business interests.

- *Organize ownership*. Advantages: better stakeholder engagement, benefit management, cost management, risk management and quality management; more efficient meetings and more support for the project.

- *Focus on products*. Advantages: clearer expectations; more stakeholder support; and less rework, hence less schedule and budget overruns.

- *Empower the project manager*. Advantages: optimum conditions for the project manager and their team; timely and efficient involvement of the steering group for strategic decision-making; and the ideal combination of motivation, flexibility and control.

The essence of all four principles is that they help you to fulfil your project sponsor role effectively and efficiently. In addition to the general leadership qualities you need, they can be seen as the building blocks of the leadership of the project sponsor.

Reverse summary: the four principles of *failing* project sponsorship

- *Don't share the business case.* Advantages: everyone can stick with their own perception of the project; during the whole project there is plenty of room for politics; and throughout the project every issue provides a new opportunity to raise fundamental discussions.

- *Don't organize business management ownership.* Advantages: the project can take on a life of its own; managers don't need to hold each other accountable; and when the project fails managers don't need to feel guilty.

- *Don't ask which specific deliverables are to be realized.* Advantages: users don't understand what happens in the project so they cannot interfere with it; supplying parties can to a large extent determine for themselves what they want to deliver; and schedule and budget overruns can remain invisible as long as possible.

- *Don't give the project manager a clear responsibility.* Advantages: you don't have to make clear when you want to be alarmed, so that your own accountability for project execution remains unclear; the project manager can easily hide setbacks; and the project can overrun its schedule without you ever having to make planning decisions for which you could be blamed.

An important advantage of all these four principles of failing project sponsorship is that no leadership qualities are required and that the status quo does not need to change.

PART TWO
Details

Introduction to Part 2

In Part 2 I discuss several aspects of project sponsorship in detail, answering numerous real-life questions. This part can be read in any order:

- Chapter 5 elaborates on the steering group: the theory sounds simple, but how does it work in practice and what pitfalls are there to avoid?

- Chapter 6 focuses on the relationship with the project manager. Should a project manager be provided by the customer's organization or by the supplier? How do you recognize a good one and how do you keep them from getting out of control?

- Chapter 7 discusses benefit management. How do you get an insight into the benefits? And, even more important, how do you create the conditions for benefit realization?

- Chapter 8 is about quality. What relevant responsibilities are there and how do you use them to achieve quality? How can you engage users effectively and efficiently in realizing quality?

- Chapter 9 is about how to deal with uncertainties. How do you ensure that risks are well controlled and how do you keep the project under control when requirements are changing?

- Chapter 10 helps you to assess documents. Are there any blind spots in this business case document? Is this plan well underpinned? Can you rely on this performance report? And is this change request well defined?

- Chapter 11 discusses the reasons projects exceed their budget and what you can do about this as a sponsor.

A closer look at the steering group

05

In Chapter 2 about the second principle, *organize ownership*, one of the main topics is the steering group as a pivot between the standing organization and the project. In many organizations there are questions about the optimum composition and the functioning of steering groups. This chapter helps you to create the conditions for a well-functioning steering group.

Who has to fulfil the project sponsor role?

Although sometimes it is obvious who should fulfil the project sponsor role, there can be many options, especially in larger organizations. When assigning the project sponsor role, the point of departure is the essence of the project's business case. The ideal project sponsor has a stronger interest than others in the realization of the business case. They feel that they are the 'owner of the business case' because the project outcome helps them to achieve their business goals. In order to be effective as chair of the steering group, the key decision-making forum of the project, the project sponsor should have a budget authority (Garland, 2009).

The key to identifying the project sponsor is not the nature of the *project deliverable*, but the nature of the *business case*. So when realizing a new theatre building, for example, with a main goal to increase the attractiveness of the theatre for the audience, the project sponsor role could be fulfilled by the director of the theatre. When realizing a new office building, with a main goal of cost reduction, the project sponsor role could be fulfilled by the facility manager.

Sometimes a number of managers share a responsibility to realize the business case. In that scenario, in order to come to a choice, check who has the largest stake, within which part of the organization the most complex or risky changes have to take place (that is where the hardest decisions are to be made), who has the most authority in the organization and who has the best capacities as a project sponsor.

Authorization

In order to realize the business case, you need to be authorized to make the required decisions. The financial margins within which a project sponsor can make decisions are called the management reserve or change budget. This enables you – in consultation with the other members of the steering group – to approve change requests. In addition to this financial authority, other authorities of the project sponsor can refer to time, quality, scope, risk or benefits. These should be defined explicitly at the start of your project: they determine your mandate – and before accepting the project sponsor role your position to discuss them is stronger than it is afterwards.

Delegating the project sponsor role

In organizations with a large project portfolio senior managers are not always able to fulfil all the project sponsor roles themselves. Indeed it might be better that they focus on the most strategic projects and delegate the sponsor roles of other projects to a subordinate. This is called 'delegated project sponsorship'. A pitfall of delegated sponsorship is that only the responsibilities are delegated, not the authorities. This has a paralysing effect on project direction, because for each relevant decision the delegated project sponsor has to turn to the 'real' project sponsor who is still pulling the strings. So when you transfer the project sponsor role, transfer it entirely, including the necessary change budget.

The sole fact that the 'real' project sponsor delegates their role to a subordinate might give stakeholders the impression that they find it less important and it can be seen as a forerunner of a failing project. In order to still create sufficient support the original project sponsor should remain visible as an unambiguous supporter of the project.

One of the risks of weak project sponsor leadership is that the project becomes at the mercy of conflicting interests, with a drifting course as a consequence. In the absence of clear direction based on the business case, users will easily increase their demands and suppliers will be readily prepared to fulfil them, with an increasing scope and cost as well as schedule overruns as a result.

Project sponsorship as a profession

In real life the picture of a line manager who owns the business case and, on top of his operational responsibilities, fulfils the project sponsor role, cannot always be maintained. Given the complexity of the project sponsor role and the competences required, more and more organizations prefer to assign this role to someone who is focused on project sponsorship as a profession. This comes in several varieties:

- The programme manager or programme director: on behalf of senior management they take on the responsibility to bring about a strategic change. Within this context they may fulfil the role of sponsor for one or more projects. In general they will cooperate closely with senior management, in order to keep them involved in relevant decisions.

- The full-time project sponsor as a function in the standing organization: an official who is fully devoted to fulfilling the sponsor role in projects. This is seen, for example, in public sector organizations with a large portfolio of construction projects. During the planning stage numerous stakeholders and interested bodies have a say, but during the execution stage this full-time project sponsor (also called project director) can operate quite independently.

- The contract management company: an external consultancy that coordinates planning, contracting and direction on behalf of the project sponsor. This is especially interesting for those organizations for whom directing projects is not their core activity, such as an insurance company that needs a new head office or a hospital that needs a new building. Many tasks of the project sponsor are taken over by the contract management company, especially guiding and controlling the contractor(s), but the project sponsor remains involved in relevant decisions.

No matter how you delegate or contract out the project sponsor role, in each case you will need to give the delegated project sponsor a fully fledged mandate, to a relevant extent larger than that of the project manager. Otherwise this arrangement is merely creating confusion about responsibilities and an extra link that slows down the chain of decision-making.

Who represents the users?

Often there is more than one candidate for the role of senior user, for example when a new working process is to be implemented in a large number of subsidiaries. Should each subsidiary be separately represented in the steering group? If so, this would make the steering group too large and therefore unworkable. Should a senior manager who is responsible for the operational management of all the subsidiaries fulfil the role? If so, this might mean that the senior user is too far removed from the environment in which the end deliverable of the project will actually be used. Choose a representative who on the one hand is close enough to the real users to ensure that user problems will directly affect their own business objectives, but who on the other hand has sufficient authority in the project environment to make informed decisions in the field of operation. In this example the senior user might be the director of one of the subsidiaries involved. But which one? Decision-making criteria could include:

- personal seniority and most authority in the organization;
- the largest number of actual users or largest turnover;
- the subsidiary most relevant to realize the benefits of the project;
- the subsidiary where the most severe implementation problems are to be expected ('if it works there, it will work anywhere').

Most likely, the managers of the subsidiaries meet regularly to discuss matters of common interest. Ideally, the manager fulfilling the role of senior user on behalf of their peers uses these regular meetings to advise and consult their colleagues about the project, so that no separate meetings are needed.

A project sponsor says...

In a consulting firm, a project focused on the development of a new service had delivered nothing useful:

'The project approach looked fantastic: all relevant departments and specialists in the organization were involved in the project, and an inventory was made carefully of all ideas and demands. The point was that we didn't come to an agreement and the final plan was an attempt to reconcile contradictory demands without making any real choices.

The proposed service lacked a clear profile, it appealed to no one. What we missed was leadership on the user side representing the customer interests, someone to cut the knot.'

More than one senior user?

In complex environments there is often a multitude of user interests: internal departments, external customers and partners, regulating bodies and so forth. Having them all take place in the steering group, however, is not a recipe for successful project direction. It will make it hard to adapt the meeting schedule to the changing needs of the project, and it will tend to make meetings last longer and go more into depth, with each representative defending their own territory instead of taking responsibility for the whole.

There are several ways to do justice to all these interests without enlarging the steering group (to be discussed further in Chapter 8). Instead, the user representation in the steering group should be as small as possible. It is up to the senior user to ensure that each user stakeholder involved gets their due influence. The senior user should in general *not* go into details such as user requirements or product quality, but oversee the project and its user environment and ensure that the project manager works with all relevant user stakeholders in order to come to a result that is really fit for purpose and acceptable to all relevant parties. This implies that a lack of detailed knowledge in the steering group of all relevant business processes in itself is not a criterion to enlarge the user representation in the steering group.

So when do you choose to add an extra user representative? In principle, only when it is unrealistic to expect that one person has sufficient credibility to represent all relevant users. In the example of the implementation of a new working process in a large number of subsidiaries this could be the case when, as a result of a recent merger or takeover, part of the subsidiaries have a substantially different cultural or operational starting position. In such a case there could be a lack of confidence in a user representative from a different background and it might be preferable to appoint senior users from both backgrounds.

A project sponsor says...

In an electronics business an automated tool was introduced to integrate sales planning and logistics in order to better align sales efforts with stock positions:

> 'The cultural gap between account management and production departments was once again confirmed. It was a challenge in itself to encourage both parties to align their operations, and it would never have been acceptable to have both parties represented by only one person. This is why we worked with two senior users from the start, who stayed in touch with their own people.'

As aforementioned, a potential pitfall of working with more than one senior user is that no one will feel responsible for the acceptance of the result by the user community as a whole. Consider appointing one of them in an overall coordinating role.

Tip for agile projects

Pay careful attention to the mandate of the product owner and their relationship to the user interests they represent. In the waterfall approach, meetings are prepared with formally documented proposed decisions and a senior user will have a strong focus on gaining support for these decisions among their grass roots before the decision is actually made. In the agile philosophy it is accepted that decisions are never perfect and that in a dynamic environment they should be made as late as possible. This requires a higher degree of authorization of the person representing the user interests, the product owner – and, at the same time, highly developed skills to still maintain grass-roots support.

Inadequate representation of user interests may lead to inadequate supervision on the usability of the products. Project performance may be very good during the execution phase as the project is 'not bothered by user intervention'. But upon completion of the project, the result proves to be insufficient or unusable, which may lead to costly reworking or the project investment being a total loss.

Who represents the suppliers?

Finally there is the senior supplier. Often, several internal and/or external suppliers are involved in a project. Not all suppliers need to be directly represented in the steering group. The question is: which supplier is the most strategically positioned? If there is a supplier who is responsible for integration of the other supplier's deliverables in the whole, such as a system integrator, this is an obvious choice. Irrespective of its actual contractual relationship (it could be an internal department), this supplier can act as the 'main contractor' and become a member of the steering group in the role of senior supplier. Outside the steering group, this supplier representative can keep in touch with the other suppliers on a one-to-one basis or organize a supplier forum in order to consider the interests of all suppliers.

Instead of taking responsibility for a project's (sub)products, suppliers can make employees available to the project on an assignment basis. If the Purchasing Department is responsible for contracting the required amount of sufficiently qualified specialists, a Purchasing Department representative could be asked to fulfil the role of senior supplier. If, on the other hand, predominantly internal employees are made available to the project on an individual basis, a manager of the department that supplies the most (scarce) employees could fulfil the senior supplier role.

A project sponsor says...

A number of subsidiaries of a concern in the machine industry was implementing software for enterprise resource planning (ERP):

'After we had selected the software package, we contracted out its implementation to a full-service ICT service provider. As the prime contractor they were responsible for integration with other business systems and their task included directing the ERP package supplier as well as the hardware supplier. As a result, this ICT service provider was the senior supplier in the steering group.

This did not work out. The bottleneck of our project soon appeared to be a lack of specialists with knowledge of the ERP package. At that stage we were fully dependent on them. It was a new package and only the package supplier could provide us with these people. At the same time, it was no longer possible to choose another ERP package and thus another supplier: the damage would have been unacceptable. The main contractor could not adequately handle the subcontractor, who was well aware of the fact that they held all the cards. In order to shorten the line of communication to the ERP supplier, we invited them to take a seat on the steering group. Formally they were indeed a subcontractor, but in reality they played a key part.'

If there is more than one senior supplier in the steering group, they should each have their own clearly defined responsibilities. Beware of a numeric majority in the steering group of supplier representatives relative to user representatives as this could endanger the business focus of the project direction.

Inadequate representation of supplier interests may lead to inadequate consideration of the feasibility of defined plans. A plan with an unrealistic budget or schedule may seem attractive to both the project sponsor and the senior user and will find easy approval, but there is little chance that it will be realized as expected.

Should an external supplier be a member of the steering group?

When a relevant part of the project is contracted out to an external supplier, one should consider whether or not to involve the external supplier in project direction. The answer to this question depends on the nature of the responsibilities of the external supplier.

When *not to involve the external supplier in project direction*

In some projects the main deliverable can be specified exactly, allowing realization to take place based on a clear definition of scope, quality, price and delivery time. The supplier and customer, however, will often have a different perception of the project, the supplier being focused on contract fulfilment and the customer on bringing about business change.

Construction project or plant relocation project?

The realization of a manufacturing building based on a blueprint and specification is seen by the contractor as a 'construction project'. The customer, however, works on a much larger project – that is, the relocation of a production plant. This project has logistic, financial, fiscal, legal, staffing, communication and technical aspects. As a part of this project, a blueprint and specification of the new building are developed, the realization of which is contracted out. After delivery by the contractor, the customer has to do a lot more before the project is completed, such as furnishing, moving and deployment.

To bring about business change the customer might establish a project organization, but it is not necessary to involve the supplier (the contractor of the main deliverable) in its direction. Thus no representative of the external supplier will be invited to take place in the steering group of the customer's project. An internal supplier will take on the role of senior supplier. They are responsible for the contract relationship with the external supplier and must ensure that they meet their obligations (contract management). They are also responsible for the availability of other external and internal resources.

Obviously, project management on the customer side is in the hands of a project manager made available by the customer organization, who directs the contractor (and other external suppliers if applicable) at an operational level. The contractor in turn will probably organize the execution of the contracted work as a project. It is up to the contractor, based on their own business case, to establish the direction and management of this construction project.

The opposite of an external supplier delivering a predefined result is a supplier who is only responsible for the quality of the specialists or materials deployed. Also in this case it basically has no added value to involve a supplier representative in the direction of the project as a steering group member. Let an internal supplier representative fulfil the role of senior supplier, for instance the one who is responsible for contracting the external specialists. This internal senior supplier should ensure that the external supplier meets its obligations.

When to involve the external supplier in project direction

Sometimes at the start of a project there is no clear picture of the end deliverable to be realized. In the case of innovation projects, even the kind of solution to be achieved and the ambition level can be uncertain. During project execution there is growing insight in opportunities and requirements, and the ambition level is influenced by the possibilities and the constraints of technology. Elaborating specifications is part of the project. You will not select a supplier based on the price of a specified product, probably not even merely on its tariffs, but to a large extent based on its vision, capabilities and references.

Business model innovation

An example is a consultancy working on business model innovation together with representatives of the sponsoring organization and its supply chain partners, with the aim to achieve carbon neutrality of the product life cycle. At each stage in the process the business case will need to be evaluated and new stakeholders may need to be engaged.

In this kind of project there is growing insight in the relationship between costs and benefits. The input of the supplier during project realization is indispensable in order to develop and adjust the business case step-by-step, which may in turn lead to adjustment of project goals. Project success highly depends on a joint effort and a one-sided approach to hold the supplier accountable to deliver a specified result will be counterproductive. No matter under what conditions the contracting out takes place: in these situations close cooperation with the external supplier is required. You should consider asking a representative of the external supplier to take a seat in the steering group.

Internal consultation

Of course you also need internal consultation about the project within the customer organization, in a management team or internal steering group. There are always issues to be discussed without the presence of the external supplier. Sometimes this internal consultation takes place by holding part of the steering group meeting without the external supplier representative. The external supplier, in its turn, undoubtedly has its own internal consultation about the project.

Other roles

No free rides

Projects need entrepreneurship. If you cannot do it the way it should be done, you should do it the way it can be done. This means making concessions to what you actually want – and this requires a balanced trade-off between all interests. In this process it is not advisable to have people on board in the steering group in roles other than the three basic ones: project sponsor, senior user and senior supplier. Indeed, if they don't have any specific responsibility for project success, they can block decisions without suffering the consequences and thus easily become a millstone around one's neck. *Un*desirable reasons for steering group membership are:

- 'In order to check quality': this can be done more efficiently in a role as product reviewer or quality inspector. A person in such a role can advise the responsible steering group member.

- 'In order to bring in knowledge': it is better to bring knowledge directly into the project team, so that the team can use the knowledge right away.

- 'In order to be informed': this is not a valid reason to burden a decision-making meeting, there are other forms of communication to achieve this.

- 'In order to watch over something', such as compliance to legal, financial, security or ICT standards: these are typically project assurance roles, for specialists, independent of the project manager, and advising the responsible steering group member.

It is the steering group that is responsible for project success and hence for decision-making, supported by the aforementioned advice. Based on a business trade-off the steering group can deviate from such advice. The rule of thumb is: no one on the steering group who has no specific responsibility. In other words: no free rides in the steering group.

Project assurance

As discussed in Chapter 2, steering group members, in combination with their joint responsibility for the success of the project as a whole, each have a specific responsibility for certain aspects of the project result. In order to carry out this responsibility they can delegate project assurance tasks.

What kind of project assurance tasks can a steering group member delegate?

Project assurance on behalf of the project sponsor (business assurance)

The project sponsor can delegate project assurance tasks:

- to make sure that the business case is used as the basis for decision-making on change requests;
- to scrutinize the risk register, the issue register, project accounts and performance reports.

Project assurance on behalf of the senior user (user assurance)

The senior user can delegate assurance tasks to check:

- the correctness, unambiguity and clarity of user requirements;
- the impact of change requests from a user perspective;
- that the right users are involved in quality reviews;
- the correctness of the recordings of quality control activities in the quality control measurements (quality register);
- that agreements about benefit realization are adhered to and that the benefit owners take their responsibilities.

Project assurance on behalf of the senior supplier (supplier assurance)

The senior supplier can delegate assurance tasks to check:

- adherence to relevant technical standards;
- that the right quality reviews are held;
- compliance of the project's deliverables to specifications;
- compliance of all suppliers involved in the project to the customer's quality system, which may contain standards for suppliers regarding the certification, qualification of staff, references and solvability.

Separation of responsibilities

A condition for successful assurance is that the relevant roles are independent of operational responsibilities. In line organizations this starting point is common property, reflected in the independent positions of auditors, internal accountants and quality assurance departments. Surprisingly in project organizations, where the risks are relatively high given the unique character of projects, less attention is paid to the separation of assurance and operational responsibilities. Known real-life examples are:

- a steering group member who combines their steering group membership with an operational role in the project team;
- a project manager who is seen as a member of the steering group instead of just participating in its meetings;
- a project office that supports the project managers and at the same time is responsible to report to senior management on the status of projects.

In all these examples, people are expected to assure the result of what is at least partially their own work. This is contradictory to the principle of independent assurance. This is not wrong per se, because you don't need to assure everything independently and you don't always have to separate responsibilities. But if you accept this, you should be aware of the risk of failing assurance.

Advisory bodies

In addition to the steering group and the project team, project organizations may contain one or more advisory bodies on behalf of users such as sounding-board groups, user reference groups and so on. If such bodies give advice to the steering group this may lead to confusion about the responsibility of the senior user: can the latter effectively make decisions, yes or no? What should the steering group do when the advice of the sounding-board group deviates from the senior user's viewpoint? This undermines the senior user's authority, its ultimate consequence being that no one can be held accountable for ensuring the quality delivered.

It is getting even worse when the status of such a group, instead of advising, is decision-making. The steering group can then become a hostage of stagnating decision-making in the sounding-board group. Can the project continue if the sounding-board group has not come to a unanimous viewpoint? The best thing to do is to give these kinds of bodies an *advisory* role and to have them advise *to the senior user*, who remains responsible to express an unambiguous viewpoint on behalf of the users in the steering group, giving the advice of the advisory board its due weight.

Change control board

The responsibility to evaluate and approve or reject change requests can be delegated to a change control board. In order to be effective, a change control board should have an explicit mandate (at least a change budget) and it is advisable that it represents relevant stakeholder groups. The responsibility to give guidance to the change control board can lie with the project sponsor or be delegated to the senior user, depending on the kind of trade-offs that the board is expected to make and the extent of their budget. In either case it should be clear to all involved who is accountable for the functioning of the change control board.

Summary

This chapter discussed several aspects of steering group composition and functioning. Link the responsibilities of steering group members as closely to their existing accountabilities in the line organization as possible. Only let an external supplier be a steering group member if you need them to develop the business case together step by step during project realization. Don't allow people to participate in steering groups without specific individual responsibilities (no free rides). If stakeholders are organized in advisory bodies, see to it that the steering group member responsibilities remain intact.

Directing the project manager

06

The fourth principle, *empower the project manager*, defines the kind of responsibilities and authorities that a project manager should be given. But where should the project manager come from, the project sponsor's organization or the supplier? And how do you recognize a good project manager? How do you clearly demarcate their responsibilities? And, last but not least, when needed, how do you exercise effective control over the project manager? That is what this chapter is about.

Who provides the project manager?

The daily management of project execution should be in the hands of one person, the project manager. Should this project manager come from the project sponsor's organization or from the supplier's organization? Both options have their pros and cons, and the answer to the question depends on the nature of the project.

Pros and cons

A project manager from the customer side (from the business environment) can have several advantages:

- They have more affinity with the business case and, based on this, are better able to make the right proposals to the steering group.

- They are better acquainted with the organization that will use the results of the project, better able to find the right people and information in this organization, and better able to use their influence in this organization, which enables them to do their work without appealing too often to the senior user.

- They can independently control the way of working of the supplier, which reduces the need for specific project assurance arrangements for supplier management.

A project manager from the supplier's side can have other advantages:

- They have more experience with the deliverables to be realized, the techniques to be used and the kind of project in general.

- They have shorter communication lines to the management of the supplier organization, are better able to find the right people and information in this organization, and better able to use their influence in this organization, which enables them to do their work without appealing too often to the senior supplier.

Considerations

Several considerations influence the choice. First, where lies the main challenge? If it lies in project execution, such as in the case of the construction of a new drilling platform, it is obvious that the supplier provides the project manager. If it lies in the implementation in the customer organization, however, as in the case of the introduction of a new ICT-system, you might prefer a project manager from the customer organization.

If you work with a project manager from the supplier side, ensure that there is a liaison at the customer side, for instance the senior user, for daily consultation and getting into contact with the right people at the user side. In addition, pay attention to supervision of project execution (project assurance) on behalf of the project sponsor.

If you work with a project manager from the customer side, most likely the supplier will deploy someone to manage the supplier side of the project. Although within many supplier organizations this person will also be called the project manager, they should report to the customer's project manager.

How do you recognize a good project manager?

In most larger organizations someone is responsible for the quality of project management and project managers: a head of the Project Management Office, a manager of the Project Management Department or similar. In principle all project managers within an organization should be at a basic competence level.

Standards

A certification based on a formal standard can help to prove the competence level of a project manager. Internationally the most relevant qualification scheme for project managers is held by the Project Management Institute, the largest international professional membership association for project managers. They issue several certificates,[1] among which are:

- Certified Associate in Project Management (CAPM®), for project team members;

- Project Management Professional (PMP®), for project managers with at least three years of project management experience;

- PMI Agile Certified Practitioner (PMI-AC®), for those working on agile projects with at least one year of agile experience;

- Program Management Professional (PgMP®), for programme managers with at least four years of project management experience and four years of programme management experience.

The first three of these certifications are based on a multiple-choice examination and hence confirm that the holder of the certificate was possessed of a certain knowledge at the moment of examination. The last certificate, PgMP, is also based on a panel review.

A certificate is an indication that the holder takes their profession seriously. Of course it is not a guarantee, and there are also good project managers without certificates.

In the United Kingdom and various other countries project management certificates based on PRINCE2 are popular: PRINCE2 Foundation (basic knowledge of the method) and PRINCE2 Practitioner (applied knowledge of the method). Both certificates require no practical experience and are based on a multiple-choice examination.[2]

However, since the final accountability for project success is yours as a project sponsor, you will also have to take responsibility for the quality of project management and for your cooperation with the project manager. Presuming that a candidate has the required formal qualification level and good personal and managerial skills, what other points of consideration are there at the intake of a project manager?

Knowledge of the environment

An adequate knowledge of the environment in which the project is to be realized and in which the result is to be used provides a relevant advantage. An insight into organization culture and history, and into the human and hierarchical relationships, makes it easier to communicate and to anticipate possible resistance. Being well informed about valid procedures in areas such as budgeting, resource allocation, risk management, quality assurance and performance reporting helps a project manager not to waste unnecessary time on these and to focus on the project itself and its stakeholders.

Knowledge of the business content

A project manager does not need to solve the business content issues of the project themselves, but the communication with stakeholders will benefit from knowledge of this content, such as logistics or marketing. This content knowledge will also help the project manager to understand where the cause of a problem lies and may contribute to their credibility.

Knowledge of relevant technology

Knowledge of the technology – such as construction technology or information technology – will help the project manager to fathom proposals from the supplier side, to assess schedules and budgets, and to oversee technical risks. In small projects, where a project manager works directly with specialists, sometimes in a role as active foreperson, technological knowledge is required. Especially in large, complex projects with a multitude of applied technologies a project manager will have to rely on others for at least part of the technological knowledge and will mainly focus on management of the process.

Creating transparency in choices to be made

A good project manager does not accept an assignment without thinking. They will want to know why you want to have the project realized, and discuss with you how the proposed solution (the project result) can best contribute to the proposed outcome (the business result). You may expect critical questions about the business case and probably about the preferred solution you have in mind. Based on their understanding of the business case a good project manager will create transparency in the choices to be made in the course of the project ('if you decide A, the consequence will be B').

Taking responsibility implies making demands

A good project manager will take responsibility for the feasibility of the project. This is only realistic when they are allowed to make demands regarding the conditions, such as the clarity of the assignment and the available time and resources. Ask the project manager if they consider the project to be feasible and under what conditions. If, at the time of an intake, the project manager does not have a sufficiently clear picture of this feasibility, you can make an agreement on when they will be able to let you know.

What type of project manager?

Not all projects equally allow to clearly define an end deliverable in advance. Be clear about your expectations. Do you really expect a project manager to accept responsibility for the delivery of a predefined result? Or do you rather expect them to apply their management skills in a process that sometimes may be fuzzy rather than planned?

The project manager in relationship with the project sponsor

When selecting a project manager the relationship with the project sponsor is of great interest. This is not only about a personal fit: given the many-sided challenge of a project it can be beneficial if you have complementary competences to the project manager. If, for example, you feel more at ease with visionary prospects, you might want to look for a project manager with an eye for details. If you feel more acquainted with facts and figures, you might be better off with a project manager with a strong focus on people.

How do you empower the project manager?

In order to be able to carry their responsibility, the project manager needs authorities:

- to accept project team members who have been assigned to the project, or at least have the right to veto them;
- to assign tasks to available project team members;
- to take corrective action within the agreed limits (tolerances).

Depending on the organization and the project, more specific authorities can be defined. In your contacts with stakeholders emphasize that the project manager's authorities are delegated authorities from the steering group (note: where this section refers to the steering group, please read: the steering group, or if there is no steering group, the project sponsor) and that the project manager acts on behalf of them.

'In our company the relationships between project sponsors and project managers used to be of a hierarchical nature. They have now developed towards a kind of contract between two parties, who both have their responsibilities.'

When preconditions and/or requirements change, the project manager may ask for additional budget or time. The steering group will then have to create a new set of circumstances in which the project manager is committed to attaining the targeted result. If no agreement can be reached, it is best to end the relationship. Continuing with a project manager who no longer believes in the project's feasibility is not a viable option.

Ultimate authority

In a results-oriented organization, the ultimate authority of a project manager is the ability to refuse or hand back their assignment.

What tolerances?

The definition of tolerances for the project manager should reflect the project's business case. In one project, for example, time may be more important than money, in another project it is the other way around. By calling tolerances 'alarm limits' you can make it easier to understand what this really is about: they are the answer to the question when you want to be alarmed right away, for instance as soon as there is one complaint from a group of customers engaged with the project.

Misunderstanding

It may seem as if granting a financial tolerance is equal to giving the project manager carte blanche to spend extra money. This is a misunderstanding. A project manager who has a tolerance of £10,000 still has to account in their performance reports for each cost overrun and each corresponding decision they made, just like when they had not agreed on any tolerance at all. Agreeing on a tolerance means that, in addition to this obligation, it is defined when they have to alarm the steering group immediately. Instead of weakening the steering group's direction of the project, the definition of tolerances strengthens it. Defining these tolerances is part of the leadership of the project sponsor.

Tip for agile projects

The agile approaches aim to reduce planning and management overhead to a minimum and rely on motivated people making the right decisions. The very short duration of the stages (iterations or sprints) with successive feedback and the short communication lines make formal tolerances superfluous. A risk of these approaches is that users and specialists, working closely together, make choices that are not in line with your business interests, for instance by realizing a product quality that is nice to have for the users but lacks tangible business value. In order to maintain the business drive of agile development, focus on the following aspects:

- Make sure that you really understand the content of the product backlog – that is, the continuously prioritized list of work items to be developed. The scope and order of the work items listed should be based on a trade-off of costs, benefits and risks in the framework of an organization's strategy. Be clear about who is authorized to change the product backlog.

- See to it that the development team resists the temptation to create solutions that are better than necessary. As a rule of thumb: the next item on the product backlog mostly has more business value than the frills of the item currently developed.

- As already said in Chapter 1: make sure that each individual involved really understands the essence of the business case, the reason why you invest in the project and what priorities follow from it.

How do you keep the project manager under control?

Trust is the basis for successful cooperation. Most project managers like to keep the steering group well informed of the project status. But between the white of reliability and the black of unreliability there are many shades of grey. Incomplete, misleading or incorrect reports may simply be caused by inexperience. Sometimes, in order to prevent 'unnecessary fuss', a project manager will not report a minor exception. In times of extreme pressure, a project manager with a good track record may be tempted to avoid mentioning a schedule overrun, because they hope or expect that soon things will start to go better – if things work out, you will never know. As a result of a strong blaming culture some project managers may hardly dare to report issues, with the effect that cost and schedule overruns are reported too late to take corrective action.

A project sponsor says...

'A project manager is only human. If you do not make demands on the project manager's planning and reporting methods, you can expect accidents to happen sooner or later and to find out about them when it is too late.'

A clear reporting and control mechanism helps to prevent derailments, but too much control can destroy motivation. The right approach most likely will be a combination of trust and control. Determine for yourself which of the measures outlined in Table 6.1 are useful within your organization and with your project manager.

Tip for agile projects

The first statement of the agile manifesto says that people and interaction are more important than processes and tools. Trust is a prerequisite for this to work. But trust does not mean that there is no control at all. In an agile approach, as an alternative to the control mechanisms listed in this section, the very short duration of the iterations – each of them followed by a meeting where the way of working is evaluated, improvements are discussed and priorities can be redefined – are the basis of control by the project sponsor.

TABLE 6.1 Measures to keep an internal project manager under control

How Can a Project Manager Become Uncontrollable?	How Can the Project Sponsor Prevent This?
Too rosy picture: to paint a more positive picture of the project's status, a project manager reports an activity or stage which is only partly complete, as complete. The resources needed to complete this activity or stage will later be reported as belonging to the next activity or stage.	Demand that each activity and stage results in a deliverable, and ask the project manager for a clear description of both the deliverable's requirements and who will test these requirements.
Unforeseen: during project execution the project manager labels some of the activities, which the steering group presumed to be already included in the project, as unforeseen, and uses them as a reason to ask for more time and/or money.	This means that the project scope is ambiguous. Have the project's end result described as a deliverable with a sufficiently accurate description of the quality requirements and how to demonstrate/prove their realization. The project scope includes all activities needed to realize this deliverable, unless explicitly stated otherwise.
Creating an undisclosed fund: the project manager includes a number of entries in the project planning and budget that are not clearly understood by the steering group, thereby creating a handy undisclosed fund for themselves to spend as they wish. In doing so, the project manager adds an 'extra tolerance' to the tolerances assigned by the steering group.	Critically approach all activities listed in the plan that have either vague descriptions (such as 'aligning', 'checking', 'preparing', 'reporting') or technical names (such as 'information analysis'). Demand that each planned activity leads to a deliverable with a purpose that is understandable to non-experts and has clear quality requirements.

How Can a Project Manager Become Uncontrollable?	How Can the Project Sponsor Prevent This?
	For general costs such as project management (the project's overhead) it is acceptable to present them as an extra item on top of these deliverable-oriented items. These overhead items can be checked based on a comparison with other projects.
Work in progress: activities in progress represent a large part of the total current stage, which makes your understanding of the status of the total stage unreliable.	Demand a plan in which activities in progress never constitute more than a limited percentage of the total scope of the stage. If there are too many activities in progress at the same time, they should be split up into smaller activities, which are to be completed individually. Each activity in itself should aim for the realization of a deliverable with quality requirements to be verified by one or more reviewers accepted by the steering group.
Gaining back time or money: the project manager reports that they are behind schedule, but that they still expect to make it to the final delivery date. In other words: they assume that the factors causing the overrun will not occur in the future and, even more, that during the remaining stages or activities of the project they will gain back as much time as has been lost so far. For the steering group this is nice to hear, but unfortunately it is not credible. The same applies to budget overruns.	A realistic starting point is: if the schedule for part of the project has been overrun, similar overruns will occur during the rest of the project. This starting point is valid until it has been proven to be invalid. What are the root causes of the overrun? What role can these factors play in the remaining stages and activities? What measures have been taken to eliminate these factors and are they demonstrably effective? Has the risk analysis been updated? What conclusions can be made about the quality of the schedule or budget?

(Continued)

TABLE 6.1 (*Continued*)

How Can a Project Manager Become Uncontrollable?	How Can the Project Sponsor Prevent This?
	Only if these questions have been answered satisfactorily may it be possible to conclude that the deviation was an isolated incident. But even then there is no reason to assume that the time or money lost will be gained back during the remaining part of the project. If the project manager claims the latter, this raises new questions. Did the original schedule contain too much slack? Was the original budget based on an overestimate?
Technical language: the project manager's use of technical language makes it hard for the steering group members to understand what is happening on the project.	Demand that all reports are written in a way that is understandable to all members of the steering group. The project manager should adapt their language to the composition of the steering group and not the other way round.
No overall picture: the project manager reports a large number of different statuses for different activities. Some activities are ahead of schedule and others are behind, some activities are over budget and others are under budget. This makes it difficult to get an overall picture.	Always ask for a consolidated report. There are techniques to present a consolidated picture of the project, in time as well as in money, which can be looked over in one glance.[3] Tip: ask the project manager to give an explicit statement in each report about whether they still think it is feasible to complete the project or stage in time.
Doubts about the reliability: it is not clear what the project manager's statements are based on. The relevance and accuracy of reports are dubious.	Get a knowledgeable professional, independent of the project manager, to check the underpinning of the reports (project assurance).

How Can a Project Manager Become Uncontrollable?	How Can the Project Sponsor Prevent This?
Only out-of-pocket costs: in the event that a project is partly carried out by internal employees the project manager bases the financial budget on out-of-pocket costs only. Internal effort is mentioned in terms of numbers of hours to be spent. The organization's total project costs are thus underestimated.	Demand that the internal costs are represented in the financial budget. If necessary, create clarity about the costs of internal hours or get the project manager to work with estimated costs. In addition to (but not instead of) an overview of the out-of-pocket costs, demand an overview of the total costs.
'The team is working very hard': the report of the past period contains a catalogue of activities making clear or suggesting that the team is very busy and is working very hard.	Demand a focus on deliverables that are realized and approved and that were mentioned in the plan. Ensure that for each deliverable realized the project manager reports its actual delivery date and its planned delivery date. When activities are reported that are not related to planned deliverables, this raises two fundamental questions: 1) shouldn't the project manager have raised a change request? 2) what is the impact of these apparently unplanned activities on the feasibility of the project's budget and schedule?

How do you keep an external supplier's project manager under control?

The same principle that applies to an internal project manager also applies to an external project manager: if there is no trust, you should not take the plunge together. All of the risks listed in the previous section apply to this situation too. When working with an external supplier's project manager, it is important to realize that there is a difference in business interests. An external project manager can be pressurized by their company to cover up problems or to create extra commercial opportunities, which makes some of the aforementioned risks even bigger, such as labelling activities as unforeseen in order to get more budget. A general preventive measure could be to appoint someone from your own organization to be your day-to-day liaison with the project manager and to play a supervising role.

TABLE 6.2 Measures to keep an external supplier's project manager under control

How Can an External Supplier's Project Manager Become Uncontrollable?	How Can the Project Sponsor Prevent This?
Additional work: when offering additional work there is practically no competition. The estimate for the additional work substantially exceeds the amount that would have been claimed if the same activities had been part of the original tender. This is why it can be very attractive for contractors to start with incomplete and imperfect specifications.[4]	Make sure that the senior user and all others involved in your organization realize that at the time of tender your negotiating position is many times stronger than afterwards. This means that it is very beneficial to have the specifications as complete as possible at the time of tender. 'We will work this out later' can be an extremely expensive statement.
Fixed price *and* time and material: the project manager of an external professional service supplier (ICT providers, management consultants, engineering contractors, etc) is executing a project on the basis of a fixed price. They can improve the metrics of this project by getting the project employees to work on time and material (T&M) activities in addition to working on the contracted project. These employees can at least 'round off' the booking of their hours to favour the project. Hours that are not clearly related to a specific part of the project (such as hours for general meetings) can easily be interpreted as hours that do not belong to the contracted project and can therefore be charged separately.	It is not advisable to let the same external employees perform activities that are part of a fixed-price project at the same time as T&M activities. Employees of commercial service providers are put under pressure to clock as many chargeable hours as possible. Where possible, at least ask the supplier to appoint separate employees for any additional T&M tasks. But even then the employee who is working on a T&M basis can help out their colleagues who are working on a fixed-price assignment at the expense of the customer organization. Engaging the same supplier under both types of agreement will always leave one open to this risk.

TABLE 6.2 (Continued)

How Can an External Supplier's Project Manager Become Uncontrollable?	How Can the Project Sponsor Prevent This?
Putting out to tender stage by stage: the supplier offers to carry out the first stage at less than the going rate so as to win the project, before (more than) recovering these costs in the following stages when it is no longer possible to switch to another supplier without incurring significant costs.	Preferably put out to tender the project as a whole and include conditions that allow you to end the cooperation after each stage. The supplier will have to indicate the assumptions on which their offer is based and, of course, will request that they can adjust their offer at the start of a new stage when new information contradicts their assumptions.
	To prevent a lock-in, define (generally accepted) requirements that the supplier has to comply with. Demand that a stage be completed in such a way that the results are transferable. The documentation of intermediate deliverables should be part of these deliverables. Check the quality plan in this respect.

Summary

This chapter has looked in detail at directing the project manager. The choice between a project manager provided by the supplier or by the customer's organization depends on the nature of the project. As least as important are the personal qualities of the project manager and their knowledge of the environment, the business content and the technology. Define clear authorities for the project manager in order to enable them to take corrective action. Whether a project manager becomes uncontrollable depends to a large extent on the demands you make and the conditions you provide as a project sponsor.

Notes

1   Based on the Project Management Body of Knowledge (PMBOK), which served as a framework for this book.

2   Issued by Axelos Ltd (its predecessors are better known: the British Office of Government Commerce, respectively the British Cabinet Office).

3   Earned value management, see the *Project Management Body of Knowledge* (PMI, 2013a).

4   A popular expression in the Dutch contracting industry is: 'additional work is written with a fork'.

Realizing the benefits

07

Most project management methods pay little or no attention to benefit management. Benefit realization is often seen as a concern after the project. The foundation for successful benefit realization, however, should be laid during the project, when developing and changing the business case. If no one feels responsible to realize the benefits that are the basis of your business case, your business case might appear to be wishful thinking. This implies that benefit management starts at the beginning of the project when the business case is developed.

Tip for the PRINCE2 environment

PRINCE2 defines that a benefit review plan should be made as a result of the process 'Closing a Project'. Effective benefit management, however, requires the creation of benefit ownership. This should best begin during the process 'Starting Up a Project' (for instance in a project board start-up meeting) to be refined and confirmed during 'Initiating a Project' and maintained whenever the business case is updated, at stage transitions or changes.

The benefit review plan defined by PRINCE2 is often interpreted as a separate document. Consider including this information in the regular performance measurement arrangements.

Whether supported by your project manager or by another professional, as a project sponsor it is in your interest to create the right conditions for benefit realization. This chapter will help you to come to a better understanding of the benefits, how to realize them and how to use benefit management to further engage your stakeholders. The best compass for project direction is a clear focus on its main benefit(s). And benefits are the most inspiring part of a business case.

Project sponsors often are dependent on others to have all the benefits realized. For instance: a division manager is the sponsor of a project in which several divisions are involved, and for which part of the benefits should be realized in other divisions. Even then the project sponsor is fully responsible for ensuring the proper application of benefit management, in order to have the managers of the other divisions involved to know and accept their responsibilities. This is why benefit management is closely related to stakeholder engagement. As discussed in Chapter 2, the senior user can play a vital role in organizing benefit management.

How do you create benefit ownership?

Benefit

A benefit is an outcome of change perceived as positive by a stakeholder. It can be financial or non-financial. Effective realization of the benefits is the ultimate goal of the project seen from the project sponsor's perspective.

Often benefits are achievements for which line management is responsible. Most benefits are relative improvements such as 'shorter delivery times' or 'increased safety'. Some benefits are absolute (true or not true) such as 'compliance to regulations'.

Concerning the extent to which the benefit is predictable, there are three types of benefit:

- *calculated benefits*, whose realization is highly predictable, such as a lower use of energy as a result of an isolation project;

- *expected benefits*, based on a professional estimate but mainly dependent on what we undertake to realize them, such as increased efficiency as a result of the introduction of new working processes;

- *ambitions*, the term we use when our intentions are conflicting with the intentions of other parties such as competitors, as is the case with a benefit like 'increased market share', or in other situations where behaviour of other parties have a strong influence on our achievements.

Benefit modelling helps us to visualize the value creation process, the individual responsibilities stakeholders have in this process and their interdependencies in a benefit map.[1]

CASE STUDY   International Domestic Appliances (1): from assumptions to commitment

A division of International Domestic Appliances is confronted with dropping business results. Investigations show that their customer satisfaction is lower than their competitors'. Customers among other things complain about long delivery times. The logistics manager proposes to start a project aiming at integration of logistic processes. This should lead to shorter delivery times. Her proposal – an outline business case – shows that it is a worthwhile investment. This conclusion is based on a number of assumptions, including the following:

- The integration of logistic processes reduces the average delivery time from 10 to 4 days.

- As a result of this, customer satisfaction – measured as net promoter score (NPS)[2] – will rise 30 per cent.

- This leads to higher turnover, which in its turn has a positive effect on the business result of €500,000.

But assumptions are no strings attached. What counts is effective benefit realization. Therefore a workshop with stakeholders is held in order to subject these assumptions in the business case to closer investigation. The participants soon realize that these assumptions should not be seen as assumptions because it is their own achievements that are at stake, namely the realization of certain benefits. Indeed, the logistics manager is responsible for the delivery times, the operations manager is responsible for customer satisfaction, the sales manager is responsible for the turnover and the division manager is responsible for the business result. Instead of assumptions, what are needed are concrete commitments.

Benefit ownership

The commitment of an individual accepting the responsibility to contribute to a joint goal by achieving a specific benefit is called *benefit ownership*. Benefit ownership is the cornerstone of benefit management.

Workshops

In many cultures this benefit ownership cannot simply be imposed upon people: it works best when people *feel* responsible. The most important condition for this is that people are able to connect to the goal of the project. In order to achieve this it is important to allow stakeholders to influence the way the goal is formulated, or at least to influence the way the goal is to be realized. For this purpose, workshops are a suitable way of working. In a benefit modelling workshop, by creating a benefit map together, stakeholders gain insight into the joint value creation process that is the basis of the business case and discover how they can realize the benefits of the business case as a joint effort by each taking their individual responsibility.

Benefit mapping

A benefit map shows what benefits are to be realized and how they depend on each other. It is advisable to have each benefit to be accompanied by the name of the person who takes responsibility for its realization, the benefit owner. The fact that the benefits are not anonymous helps us to prevent wishful thinking. Indeed, when an expected benefit is unrealistic, the benefit owner concerned has a good reason to oppose it. Adding names to benefits also makes clear that the realization of the business case is not a matter of calculation but of people working together.

In a benefit map, arrows express dependencies, but not necessarily cause–effect relationships. A -> B means that when A grows, B can grow as well, but this might require action from the benefit owner of B. By working on a benefit map together, the participants learn from each other how the value creation process works and how their individual achievements contribute to it. This benefit map, including benefit owners and dependencies, is a good foundation for further elaboration of the business case.

CASE STUDY   International Domestic Appliances (2): a benefit map

The participants summarize their commitments and mutual dependencies in a benefit map as presented in Figure 7.1.

FIGURE 7.1   The benefit map drafted by the participants of the workshop

The benefit map makes clear how each person depends on others when contributing to the whole. Only through cooperation can they achieve a good result together. The benefit map also makes clear that customer satisfaction not only depends on delivery time: also relevant are product quality, on-time delivery and service. Investments in the reduction of delivery time should hence be weighed against possible investments in other factors that influence customer satisfaction.

Specifying the benefits

Before you can make these commitments more concrete, you need to agree on their definitions and how to measure them.

CASE STUDY   International Domestic Appliances (3): definitions and criteria

As a result of their workshop the participants come to an agreement on the following definitions and criteria:

- Product quality: the percentage of products delivered correctly the first time.

- Delivery time: the average time between the moment when the customer places the definite order and the moment when the customer is physically in possession of the ordered product.

- On-time delivery: the percentage of deliveries of which the actual delivery time is equal to or shorter than the delivery time agreed with the customer.

- Service: to be decided.

- Image: to be decided.

- Customer satisfaction: satisfaction of the customer with the company as a whole expressed in net promoter score (NPS).

- Turnover: equal to annual report.

- Business result: equal to annual report.

This overview of benefits makes clear that most benefits are of a non-financial nature. In this example the final benefits – a higher turnover and a better business result – are of a financial nature.

The next step is to quantify the benefits.

CASE STUDY International Domestic Appliances (4): expected benefits and ambitions

After having done some homework to explore these benefits and what is needed to realize them, in a second workshop the participants come to define a number of concrete commitments:

- The reduction in delivery time can be predicted to a reasonable extent. The logistics manager accepts the responsibility to realize an average delivery time of four days after execution of the project.

- The effect of this on the customer satisfaction is harder to predict. Based on a reduction of delivery times to four days, the operations manager takes on the ambition to increase customer satisfaction by 20 per cent (according to him 30 per cent is unrealistic).

- Based on a 20 per cent increase of customer satisfaction, the sales manager takes on the ambition to increase turnover by 10 per cent, with a delay of six months.

- Based on a 10 per cent increase of turnover, the division manager increases the target for the business result by €400,000.

A summary of the expected financial benefits, based on the specific commitments and ambitions of managers involved, is presented in Table 7.1. These benefits are calculated for three scenarios:

- worst-case: if all circumstances (such as market developments) are unfavourable;

- most likely: assuming most probable circumstances;

- best-case: if all circumstances (such as market developments) are favourable.

TABLE 7.1 Proposed financial benefits

Effect on Business Result Per Year	Worst Case	Most Likely	Best Case
As a result of higher turnover	+ €150,000	+ €400,000	+ €900,000
As a result of lower operational cost (not included in the benefit model presented)	+ €100,000	+ €100,000	+ €100,000
Total benefits per year	+ €250,000	+ €500,000	+ €1,000,000

NOTE The figures refer to the difference between the benefits of investing (executing the project) and not investing (the zero option – that is, continuing without changing anything).

By underpinning the business case this way (with benefit owners, quantification and relating financial to non-financial benefits), you realize that it is not an expectation with no strings attached, but that it is connected as closely as possible to concrete responsibilities and the ambitions of stakeholders.

Tip for agile projects

When discussing priorities in the product backlog the following typical benefit management questions may help you to separate the wheat from the chaff:

- What benefits can we achieve when this work item is realized?
- Who is committed to realize these benefits?

How do you direct benefit realization?

In most cases, projects don't deliver benefits by themselves, nor can benefits be harvested like ripe fruit ready to be picked. The benefits of a project often are the outcome of change that is the result of hard work by (some of) the stakeholders, enabled by the deliverables of the project. This change seldom takes place exactly according to plan, and the outcome is often hard to predict. If this is the case, then why would we make a plan for the realization of the benefits, a benefit realization plan? A benefit realization plan is a *summary of the expectations and ambitions of stakeholders*. It consists of one or more benefit map(s) (containing, amongst others, the names of the benefit owners) and, in addition, information about the size of the proposed benefits and when those involved expect to realize them.

Such a benefit realization plan is not intended to be a straitjacket, but to be a baseline for stakeholders to assess the actual effects of their behaviour. A benefit realization plan indicates what achievements are to be made and when. As such it is a yardstick for performance measurement. The differences between plan and measurement are the trigger for discussion among stakeholders in order to further improve their understanding of the value creation process and a trigger for corrective action.[3]

In addition, the benefit realization plan, combined with the investment plan, offers relevant information for elaboration of the business case. When the project is part of a programme, the timeline of benefits to be realized is input for defining programme stages (also called tranches).[4]

Measuring performance, learning and taking corrective action

Measuring the achievements of benefit realization against plan only provides data. These data only become meaningful when stakeholders interpret them and transfer them into information and, based on this, come to a joint insight into the working of the value creation process and decide to take corrective action to further improve this. Therefore the key to successful performance measurement does not lie in the gathering of data itself, but in a social process of interaction between people with complementary knowledge. For this reason it is often useful, also after completion of the project, to organize a few benefit management workshops focused on the transfer of benefit measurement into action.

CASE STUDY International Domestic Appliances (5): measuring benefit realization, learning and taking corrective action

Three months after completion of the project the first figures about delivery times and customer satisfaction, related to the new situation, are available. About turnover and business result no relevant new data are available yet. The managers involved convene in order to discuss the progress of benefit realization and if necessary to decide on corrective actions.

It appears that the proposed delivery time reduction from to days has been largely realized: it now comes to an average of five days. The logistics manager considers that, when all employees are well used to the new working process, some more fine-tuning will be possible in order to indeed realize the intended four-day delivery time.

The figures on customer satisfaction, however, are quite disappointing. In spite of the shorter delivery times, customer satisfaction has hardly improved. The operations manager has spoken to a number of customers about this. It appears that they are disappointed about the result because they had expected more, based on communication about the expected improvements. A delivery time of five days is not enough for someone who expects four days. And on top of that five days is just an average; sometimes orders are delivered in four days, but it appears that 30 per cent of the orders are not delivered on time – that is, not within the time agreed with the customer.

The team comes to the conclusion that communication about the improvements has been inaccurate, and that although the delivery times have been significantly improved, on-time delivery is now the bottleneck. The team therefore decides to take the following actions:

- The marketing manager takes on the responsibility to improve communication with customers about the new working process and what they can expect from them in order to prevent too high expectations.

- The operations manager takes on the responsibility to improve communication with individual customers about specific orders, so that they will have realistic information about the expected delivery times of their orders.

- For the coming period the logistics manager takes on the responsibility to pay extra attention to on-time delivery. They want to raise this to 95 per cent.

The team decides to meet again in two months' time, when the first effects of these actions should be visible.

As soon as you are convinced that benefit realization and its meas-urement (for example by including it in the regular key performance indicators of the organization) has become part of business as usual, it is not useful any more to separately measure and report the benefits of the project.

The motivating force of benefit management

In a dynamic environment we can only turn projects into a success if we avail ourselves of opportunities, are flexible and keep adapt-ing ourselves to new circumstances. This requires that people take responsibility, come with ideas and take initiatives, and hence that they are truly motivated. Research collected by Daniel Pink (2009) indeed shows that organizations that are successful in a highly dynamic environment are organizations that appeal to the intrinsic motivation of people instead of relying on control.

According to Pink there are three sources of intrinsic motivation:

1 Autonomy: our natural inclination to self-direction.

2 Mastery: our natural need to get better at what we do (this starts with learning to walk and talk, and later is expressed in sports, hobbies and work).

3 Purpose: our longing to be part of something bigger than ourselves and to be meaningful for this (for instance to contribute to a higher cause or to be meaningful to others).

Well-applied benefit management builds exactly on these three sources:

- **Autonomy:** by working in workshops participants experience that their insights and opinions count and that they have an influence on their own role and responsibility, as opposed to a task being imposed upon them. And when they accept a responsibility as benefit owner, they experience that this responsibility is related to the outcome of their actions, leaving room for their own judgement as to the way they will achieve it.

- **Mastery**: well-applied benefit ownership aligns as closely as possible to the basic responsibility a person already has in their role as a manager, and provides them with the means to improve their achievements in their profession. For most people it feels good to improve themselves, especially when it is clear that it is their own achievement.

- **Purpose**: by working on the business case together, stakeholders can buy in to the business case. For an individual, benefit management is motivating because it relates individual achievements to the realization of the business case as a shared goal. Knowing that as an individual one contributes to a joint goal is one of the main factors that lead to a feeling of happiness on the shop floor (Van Campen, 2012).

The advantages of benefit management

Well-applied benefit management offers the following advantages:

- better underpinned and supported decisions about investments;

- a better return (financial and/or non-financial) on investments;

- a basis for empowerment, because benefit ownership combines a clear focus on outcome (effects to be reached) with agility regarding the means and the realization;

- an aid to motivate a team intrinsically by linking the individual achievements with their contribution to the shared goal;

- an aid to support business management to accept responsibility for the success of projects, which reduces the dependence on change professionals and communication specialists;

- an aid for joint learning about the value creation process;

- more sustainable success of projects by preventing resistance in the implementation phase;

- it helps people to feel part of a team, to make a joint effort and to count.

> ### Make common sense common practice
>
> The realization of benefits (positive financial or non-financial outcomes) is *the* reason to invest in change. Introducing benefit management is 'to make common sense common practice' (Bradley, 2010).

Summary

In order to come to a reliable insight into the project benefits and to realize them, you need to work closely with the project stakeholders and create benefit ownership. Working together on a benefits map helps stakeholders to come to a joint understanding of the value creation process and their individual contribution to the common goal: the realization of the business case. A benefit realization plan helps as a basis to monitor progress and to take corrective action. Well-applied benefit ownership aligns with the basic sources of intrinsic motivation, and most participants to benefit workshops consider this to be a very motivating experience.

Notes

1 A complete benefit map contains the business goal, the benefits and disbenefits, the business changes and the project deliverables. In this chapter we only discuss the benefits. For more extensive information on benefit mapping and benefit management see *Benefit Realisation Management* (Bradley, 2010).

2 Net promoter score (NPS) is an often-used yardstick for customer loyalty. Measuring NPS is based on a single question: how likely is it that you would recommend our company/product/service to a friend or colleague? Scoring for this answer is most often based on a 0 to 10 scale. Promoters are those who respond with a score of 9 or 10 and are considered loyal enthusiasts. Detractors are those who respond with a score of 0 to 6 – unhappy customers. Scores of 7 and 8 are passives, and they will only count towards the total number of respondents, but not directly affect the formula. NPS is calculated by subtracting the percentage of customers who are detractors from the percentage of customers who are promoters. Source: Wikipedia, 22 November 2014.

3 For an inspiring view on how performance measurement can be a driving force in improving organizations, see *Transforming Performance Measurement: Rethinking the way we measure and drive organizational success* (Spitzer, 2007).

4 For more information about benefit management in the context of programme management, see *The Standard for Program Management* (PMI, 2013b) or *Managing Successful Programmes* (OGC, 2007).

Achieving quality 08

The project manager, together with the users and suppliers involved in the project, is responsible for the delivery of quality. However, as discussed in Chapter 2, the accountability for the delivery of quality lies with the members of the steering group. The senior user should be held accountable for functional quality and the senior supplier should be held accountable for technical quality. But what is quality and what can you do as a project sponsor or steering group member to ensure the circumstances in which quality can be created? How can you ensure quality, without getting lost in details? How can user involvement in the process of creating quality be effective and efficient? These are the subjects of this chapter.

Tip for the PRINCE2 environment

There are some differences in terminology regarding quality management between this book and the PRINCE2 environment.

TABLE 8.1 Terminology for quality management

This Book	Corresponding PRINCE2 Term
quality management plan	quality management strategy
quality activities	quality control
quality control measurements	quality register
project scope description	project product description
high-level requirements	customer's quality expectations

What is quality?

In most accepted definitions, quality is the extent to which a product or service meets its specifications or meets the expectations of its users. ISO 9000 defines quality as the degree to which a set of inherent characteristics fulfils the requirements: requirements are defined as needs or expectations.

Control or trust

According to some, however, quality is about more than meeting needs or expectations. Robert Pirsig distinguishes between *static quality* and *dynamic quality* (Pirsig, 1991). Static quality has to do with complying with predefined requirements and standards. This is 'the quality of bookkeeping': predictable and repeatable. This type of quality can be ensured by exercising adequate control. Dynamic quality has to do with the use of creativity and the creation of something unique, unexpected. This is 'the quality of a work of art', not predictable but unpredictable, not repeatable but once only. This type of quality cannot be ensured with control; it requires creativity – for which you need to give room and trust.

In projects both types of quality can be relevant. In a project aiming at replacing all the printers in an organization the focus will be on static quality: the most important thing is that they all function according to demands. The project deliverable has the required quality when it meets these demands and can be tested objectively.

However, in a project aiming at the development of a new town hall, the development of a house style or the development of a website, the product should not only meet formal requirements. In order to be successful something unique should be created, something different from anything else existing so far. What you need are creative and engaged people who come with unusual ideas, and this requires dynamic quality.

Sometimes one phase of a project requires more dynamic quality (for example to come to a unique design) while another phase requires more static quality (to realize this design in a controlled way).

Noriako Kano makes a similar distinction between *must-be quality* (what customers expect) and *attractive quality* (what customers had not yet thought about, what exceeds their expectations) (Kano, 1996).

The power of trust

Interesting examples illustrating the power of trust over control are Linux and Wikipedia.

Linux is an open source operating system. This means that no one owns it, its code is open to anyone and anyone can change it without formal quality control. There is no budget for development, there is total transparency and people correct each other's errors. Windows is the closed source operating system developed by Microsoft at huge cost and its development is subject to tight quality control. For the most mission-critical systems many companies prefer Linux, however, precisely because of its reliability, even though there is no supplier who guarantees it.

Wikipedia is an open source encyclopaedia. Any user can directly contribute to it by adding new items or editing existing ones. Instead of formal quality control, users correct each other. Working with a minimum budget based on donations Wikipedia surpasses all other encyclopaedias in terms of alignment with user interests, up-to-dateness (when a celebrity dies, their biography is usually adjusted the same day) and extensiveness. As a result, Wikipedia has become the preferred encyclopaedia for millions of users all over the world.

What are key responsibilities regarding quality?

As said in Chapter 2 about the second principle, *organize ownership*, the application of project management processes should be left to the project manager, but the assignment of business responsibilities around the project is your concern as a project sponsor. The same is true for quality management processes and the assignment of business responsibilities regarding quality. This section helps you to understand all responsibilities related to quality in projects.

The project sponsor: accountable

As a project sponsor you are accountable for project success and, as such, for delivered quality. In order to be able to carry this responsibility effectively and efficiently, you will need to delegate the right responsibilities.

Steering group members: accountable for aspects of quality

It is advisable to delegate specific quality accountabilities to members of the steering group. A user representative should be held accountable for functional quality, including the quality of specifications and that the project deliverable can be well used, managed and maintained. A supplier representative should be held accountable for technical quality, including compliance to specifications. This implies that they are to supervise (or have supervised) the quality of the products and services delivered by the project manager and the way they are realized.

The project manager

The realization of the project deliverables and hence the realization of quality is the project manager's main responsibility. They are responsible for planning quality management – that is, to identify the quality requirements and, when applicable, relevant quality standards or policies and to include them in the quality management plan. The quality management plan describes how to control and assure quality.

During project execution the project manager is responsible for managing the quality activities, to record their results and to recommend changes when necessary for acceptance by the stakeholders. It is up to the project manager to propose how all the responsibilities defined in this section should be effectively and efficiently used in the creation of quality in a specific project. They will describe this in the project quality plan, to be approved by the steering group.

Quality reviewer: checking the quality of deliverables

Quality reviewers are people who perform quality control activities in order to check the quality of deliverables. This may include all sorts of quality activities such as the approval of requirements, the validation of a design, inspections on behalf of specific stakeholders, technical tests and acceptance tests. At least some of the quality reviewers should represent the user interests. Supervising bodies also can play this role.

The steering group is responsible for ensuring that the quality reviewers effectively represent the interests of relevant stakeholders and ensure that their findings are properly laid down and reported, as a basis for go/no-go decisions. Check if each member of the steering group knows who is reviewing quality on behalf of them and realizes that the responsibility for quality is ultimately a business responsibility.

Quality reviews should not degenerate into defining new requirements over and over again. Therefore they should be based on a clear baseline. For instance, the acceptance of a final deliverable should be based on its design, or the acceptance of a design should be based on the requirements. If a deliverable complies with its baseline but the reviewer holds the opinion that it is not fit for purpose, this should not result in the rejection of the deliverable but in a request to change the baseline.

Formal acceptance of deliverables

The results of quality control are not always unambiguous. Sometimes there are minor deficiencies not worth the rework and sometimes different reviewers have different findings. In these cases a decision is needed, since accepting the product with minor deficiencies may be preferable to postponing its acceptance until the product meets all its requirements. In this decision all relevant aspects should be taken into account, from market opportunities to legal risk, from maintenance costs to the cost of rework, from user interests to supplier interests. The steering group, representing all relevant stakeholder interests, is the appropriate body to make these trade-offs and formally accept project deliverables. Decision-making about the acceptance of specified intermediate deliverables might be delegated to the project manager.

Project assurance: supervision on behalf of the steering group

Project assurance is supervision on the way of working of the project manager by or on behalf of the steering group members. Persons in project assurance roles report to a member of the steering group independently of the project manager. This is discussed in detail in Chapter 5. Project assurance can serve to ensure that the user representatives are properly involved in quality control activities and that their findings are correctly laid down in the quality register.

Quality assurance: auditing on behalf of corporate management

Quality assurance is supervision on behalf of corporate management, often conducted by a quality assurance department or similar organization. Its aim is to ensure that the project complies with the organization's quality policy and quality system. This often takes place by means of audits, the results of which are reported to corporate management, independently of the project sponsor, the steering group and the project manager.

What instruments does the steering group have to achieve quality?

Achieving quality requires an environment in which people are motivated to deliver quality. This mainly depends on leadership and general management capabilities. Specific ways for a project steering committee to influence this are:

- Actively share the business case, to stimulate users and specialists to come with ideas for optimum solutions.

- Do not just criticize what is wrong but above all appreciate what is right and celebrate achievements, thus contributing to self-confidence and motivation of the project team.

- Empower the project manager, thus allowing the project team to take responsibility and initiative; and divide the project into management stages – that is, stages at the end of which results are accepted by the steering group, thus allowing you step-by-step to take responsibility for a quality that is acceptable for all stakeholders.

- Users are the driving force behind quality – involve them at all stages of the process, thus allowing them to influence all aspects of the result.

Project management methods contain a wide range of formal instruments for quality management. The challenge is to have these applied to an extent that suits the specific project. Well-organized quality responsibilities can help you to prevent detailed discussions in the steering group while at the same time reducing the amount of quality issues. Too extensive an application of quality management instruments leads to bureaucracy and is counterproductive. Together with steering group members and the project manager you will have to find the right balance. In this process two relevant trade-offs are to be made:

- Control versus trust. A high level of control allows you always to keep a finger on the pulse, but at the same time it hampers the creative process. It makes people spend time on justification instead of creation, it may demotivate good professionals because they don't feel trusted and it may undermine people's responsibility to deliver quality right away ('who cares, everything will be checked over and over again anyhow').

- Predictability versus ambition. Do you want to be sure to achieve an acceptable quality or are you prepared to take risks to achieve a unique quality?

Ensure that the steering group's considerations are taken into account by the project manager when drafting the quality management plan. And when selecting the project manager you may have anticipated on this: does the project primarily require a visionary project manager or someone who closely sticks to the standards and rules?

A project sponsor says...

'At the start of the project we invited the whole project team for a visit to our plant where the software would be implemented. They could see everything with their own eyes and ask their questions. They really understood the process and I believe this contributed more to the quality of the result than all the formal quality measures we demanded.'

The steering group has a number of formal instruments to achieve quality:

- high-level requirements (customer's quality expectations);
- acceptance criteria;
- project scope description (project product description);
- quality management plan (quality management strategy);
- product requirements;
- quality control measurements (quality register).

High-level requirements

High-level requirements are defined as part of the project charter (project brief). They are the framework for the quality to be realized by the project and are highly relevant to make sure that this quality will meet the expectations of sponsor and users. By paying careful attention to these requirements you prevent time being wasted on superfluous solutions and avoid getting sidetracked.

Acceptance criteria

Acceptance criteria should be defined as part of the project scope statement. These are the specific criteria that each group of stakeholders (such as users, maintenance staff, certifying bodies) will apply when accepting the final project deliverables. By accepting the criteria the steering group demarcates the finish line of the project, thus creating focus in all choices to be made by the project management team, especially those regarding scope and quality.

The high return of timely thinking

When acceptance criteria only become clear in the course of the project, this can lead to high additional costs and loss of time. Make sure that all stakeholders understand that thinking carefully about acceptance criteria can give a very high return. However, no matter how much effort you put into this, later changes to the acceptance criteria cannot always be avoided. It is up to the project manager to propose these to the steering group as change requests.

Project scope description

Since scope creep is an important cause of budget and schedule overruns (see Chapter 11), it is essential to have the scope of the project clearly defined and see to it that throughout the project it is used as the baseline for change control. The project manager should draft the project scope description together with relevant stakeholders, based on the high-level requirements and acceptance criteria, and to have it accepted by the steering group.

Quality management plan

The quality management plan describes how the organization's quality policies will be implemented and how the project management team will meet with the quality requirements set for the project.

A good quality management plan should focus on prevention and help to reduce the number of issues found in quality control activities, thus reducing the schedule and cost overruns caused by rework.

The essence of quality management in projects

The following situations are perhaps familiar:

- During the course of a project new requirements arise, causing extra work and costs.

- Resistance arises during the handover of the end result to the operational and maintenance environment.

- At the end of the project there are still many open issues and it is not clear who is going to resolve them.

- The end result does not completely meet expectations.

These are all quality issues. The purpose of the quality management plan is to prevent these issues and make sure that the project delivers what the stakeholders actually need and expect. The basic questions to be answered by a quality management plan are:

1 With what standards and specific requirements should the end result comply?

2 Who will be responsible to realize and assure this?

3 How will it be organized that the result indeed complies with these requirements and how is this going to be confirmed?

What counts is that stakeholders agree on the answers to these questions and that they are laid down and adhered to. That is the essence of quality management in projects.

Specifications

Before realizing the end deliverable of the project, numerous intermediate deliverables can be created. For steering group members, specifications are an aid to control quality without having to actually check the deliverables themselves. When approving a specification, thus defining the quality to be realized, it should also be made clear which people are authorized to test the deliverable against this specification: it is the quality reviewers, who often act on behalf of specific stakeholders. The project manager should only report a deliverable as completed after having its quality tested by the quality reviewers accepted by the steering group.

Quality control measurements

The quality control measurements contain the results of all quality control activities. If the project manager reports a deliverable as complete, this should be confirmed by the quality control measurements. The steering group can use the latter to check (or have checked by an auditor) the reliability of progress reporting.

How do you engage users in realizing quality effectively and efficiently?

Research into the causes of success and failure of projects confirms time and again that the right engagement of users is a principle success factor. Since user expectations play a key role in the definition of quality, properly focused user influence is one of the main keys to achieving quality. It not only contributes to the quality of the result, but also to the acceptance of the result, the prosperous use of the result and the realization of the proposed benefits. Unfocused user influence, however, may lead to conflicts, delays and disappointments.

Frame of reference: the business case

Each project has its constraints and not all wishes can be realized. It is therefore mostly not advisable to invite users to just express their wishes. See to it that user communication always refers to the business case as a frame of reference, in order to make sure that expectations are realistic. In an agile approach, with its strong user influence, this is even more relevant.

Managing expectations

Instead of an invitation to bring in user requirements, the essence of a proper invitation to users could be: 'The goal of our project is to achieve cost reduction in the sales process. Based on your knowledge and experience as a sales person, would you be willing to contribute to this, to make sure that the solution will really work and enable the realization of the proposed benefits?' In this way the constraints are clear from the outset, because everyone understands that wishes that do not contribute to cost reduction in the sales process may not be realistic. If it is necessary to discuss this with the users involved, it is easier to do so before they have made a lot of effort for the project rather than afterwards.

The position of users in the project

A condition for proper user participation is that those involved have a good understanding of their position in the project organization. Here, too, communication is the key. See to it that in this respect the senior user takes the relevant responsibility.

User kick-off meeting

When a large number of user representatives will be involved in quality activities, the senior user can hold a kick-off meeting especially for this group, in order to discuss their role. This should begin with an explanation of the business case as a frame of reference within which user involvement is useful. A subsequent explanation of the specific role of these user representatives in the project would contain the following key elements:

- You are responsible for checking quality on behalf of your colleagues, so be aware of the relevance of your role and the impact it might have on the whole team if you overlook issues.

- Please accept the guidance of the project manager insofar as it is related to the agenda and the process ('We have a tight schedule, would you please participate in an extra review meeting early tomorrow morning?').

- Please do *not* accept guidance of the project manager when it is related to quality itself ('We have a tight schedule, would you please approve this deliverable now?').

- I am your steering group representative and in case of a difference of opinion about quality issues I want you to contact me directly.

Make sure that everyone understands the difference between *rejecting a deliverable* (because it does not comply with its requirements) and *making a change request* (in order to change the requirements). If you also invite the project manager to this meeting, the roles of the user representatives will be clear for each one involved.

Alternatives for steering group participation

For reasons of flexibility and decisiveness it is advisable to keep the steering group as small as possible. Instead of creating extra seats for steering group members there are other ways to strengthen user influence, as shown in Table 8.2.

TABLE 8.2 Strengthening user influence

How can users influence *specifications?*	Get users to participate in or lead working groups in which specifications are developed.
	Hold a user survey to make an inventory of their ideas.
	Have a prototype made to be commented on by users.
	Hold brainstorming sessions with user groups.
	Get the users to develop (successive versions of) the design together with specialists.
	Integrate users and specialists in one team, concerned with specifications, design and realization (agile approach).

(Continued)

TABLE 8.2 (*Continued*)

How can users influence *decision-making*?	Appoint the right senior user in the steering group and ensure effective communication with their grass roots.
	Get the senior user to use operational meetings with their peers or subordinates – such as management meetings and team meetings – to gather input for decision-making.
	Organize user representatives in a user council or user reference group, chaired by the senior user. This body advises the senior user.
	Delegate decision-making on details to a team at shop-floor level with direct user participation.
How can users check the *quality of deliverables*?	Let users participate in quality control teams that check the quality of deliverables.
	Have a pilot organized for users to provisionally use a deliverable.
	Get users to participate in an acceptance test of the final deliverable.

A project sponsor says...

'When executing maintenance and renovation plans to our dwellings our approach has changed. It used to be one-way traffic, we made the plans and the tenants just had to accept them. Occasionally this led to serious conflicts.

At present we strive to get around the table with tenant representatives from the outset. We start directly with intensive communication to all tenants involved. Since they are involved in the choices that are made, the tenants show more understanding for the annoyance caused by the works and sometimes even for a possible rent increase. What it all comes down to is that we started to consider our tenants as customers and to take them seriously. As a result this kind of process now runs a lot easier and smoother, to the benefit of all.'

Summary

Quality is about meeting expectations of stakeholders, and in some projects exceeding them. The project manager is responsible for realizing quality but the accountability for quality lies with the members of the steering group, who should find the right balance between trust and control. Whereas the application of quality management processes should be left to the project manager, as a project sponsor, together with the steering group, you should focus on the proper assignment of business accountabilities and responsibilities regarding quality: those of steering group members, those of quality reviewers on behalf of the business, project assurance and quality assurance.

Dealing with uncertainties

Delivering projects and realizing business cases contains far more uncertainty than business as usual. What is driving the project is the promising outcome, the benefits: it is an opportunity and not a guarantee. However, there are many more opportunities to discover. Therefore uncertainty should not be avoided but embraced.

This chapter is about:

- risk management – anticipating events that might occur in the future and that, if they occur, have an impact on the proposed objectives of the project;
- change control – managing modifications to documents, deliverables or baselines.

Proper risk management and change control are prerequisites to being successful in a dynamic environment.

How do you ensure that risks are properly managed?

A pitfall in defining risks is that it degenerates into looking for anything that could go wrong. Thus, risk analysis becomes a purpose on its own. See to it that risk analysis is always related to the business case of the project: the question is not what could go wrong, but what could go wrong that could threaten the realization of the business case.

Overlooking the most relevant risk[1]

A large bank had started a project to introduce speech recognition in their call centre. This would enable callers, instead of having to work through a menu, to tell the computer what they wanted and be connected to the right department right away. The risk assessment, performed by the project team, had led to the definition of numerous risks, especially technical ones.

In a steering group start-up meeting one of the main items on the agenda was the business case. The business case document contained quite a list of benefits, among them:

- reduction of the number of internal transfers;

- reduction of the average call time because the subject of the call is shown directly on the screen of the call-centre employee;

- increased turnover as the subject of the call is automatically used for cross-selling purposes;

- strengthened innovative image of the bank;

- increased customer satisfaction.

The steering group members appeared to have different views on what was the driving motivation behind the project. Most of them assumed that cost reduction through reduction of the number of internal transfers and reduction of the average call time was the essence. After some discussion the project sponsor concluded that the business case document had focused on the financial justification in order to acquire the project budget. His main reason for starting the project, however, was the aim to strengthen the innovative image of the bank. A lot of customers dislike telephone menus. By connecting them to the right department faster and easier the bank could distinguish itself from its competitors and this could be utilized in publicity. This was the essence of the business case.

Later on in the meeting, when discussing the worries of the steering group members, the project sponsor said that his main worry – in line with the essence of the business case – was that a competitor would be the first on the market with the same innovation. This would to a large extent destroy the business case.

A quick review of the results of the risk assessment conducted by the project team learned that exactly this risk, of a competitor being the first, had been overlooked. Because the project team had conducted the risk assessment without a proper insight into the essence of the business case, there had been a blind spot for what in the eyes of the project sponsor was the most relevant risk. As a mitigating measure an alternative scenario was defined that could be used should a competitor announce the introduction of speech recognition. Among other things this scenario included going live sooner, with limited functionality and a supporting communication plan.

Indeed, risk management should not stand on its own but be related to the business case.

Risk management starts with risk analysis and there are basically two types of approach to risk analysis: bottom-up and top-down.

Bottom-up risk analysis

A bottom-up approach is based on the experience and knowledge of stakeholders. Structured brainstorming sessions or interviews are used to make an inventory of risks. It is essential to involve not only the project team but all categories of stakeholders (project sponsor, users, suppliers, partners, consultants), since each stakeholder has their own interests and their own blind spots. Precisely by working together they can take away each other's blind spots and come to a well-balanced risk analysis. Working with stakeholders is the best guarantee to cover all relevant aspects of the project's business case.

Support for risk mitigation measures

Risk analysis should not be a technical exercise. It is about a group of people who are facing a challenge together and openly share their concerns. This is the foundation for successful cooperation. The power of the bottom-up approach lies not only in the tailor-made result but also in the effect on team-building, commitment and support for the risk mitigation measures.

Top-down risk analysis

The top-down approach is based on checklists, recorded experience with similar projects or standard risk profiles for specific categories of projects. These are all tools that make use of the experience of previous projects (inside or outside the organization) to define the risks of a next project. Top-down risk analysis is a way to benefit systematically from errors previously made.

Risk mitigation

The project manager can use a top-down tool to check the results of a bottom-up risk analysis. A solid risk analysis is based on both approaches, top-down and bottom-up. Beware if the result of risk analysis is only laid down in a risk register or separate risk section of the project plan. If taken seriously, risk analysis leads to risk mitigation measures. If these measures cost time and money, this should be reflected in proposed changes to the project plan itself, including its schedule and budget.

Who is responsible for risk management?

As a project sponsor you are ultimately responsible for the quality of risk management. Of course the organization of risk management should be left to the project manager. In consultation with stakeholders they take care of the risk analysis and the definition of risk mitigation measures. As a part of the project management plan (project initiation documentation) the project manager submits the proposed risk management approach to the steering group. An indispensable part of any risk approach is that the current status of risks is recorded in a risk register (risk log). You can define a project assurance role to ensure that the approved risk management approach is actually executed.

See to it that for each risk the risk ownership is clearly defined – that is, the responsibility of an individual to keep an eye on the occurrence of the risk and, in case of its occurrence, to trigger the defined risk response measures. Risk ownership is best to be assigned to the one who most likely will be the first to notice. Thus a financial manager might be the owner of a risk related to changing currency rates, or a sales manager might be the owner of a risk related to negative reactions of customers.

A project sponsor says...

'The other day, for the first time, I had a steering group meeting where risk owners were assigned for each risk, exactly as the book tells you to do it. I am the owner of two risks and I have to admit that at first it didn't really feel comfortable. But I also would be the first to admit that this approach makes you feel responsible. All at once risks are no longer anonymous.'

In the steering group, make an appeal to the senior user to define user-related risks and to the senior supplier to define supplier-related risks, and hold all members to account for their responsibilities as risk owners.

Concerns

When you ask stakeholders to think about risks, they might react that risk analysis is 'something for the project manager'. Therefore, don't ask for risks, but ask: what are your main concerns about this project? This usually leads to better answers. When a project team has conducted a risk analysis, and after that you ask the steering group members what their concerns are, the latter often leads to relevant additions to the risk analysis.

Steering group decision-making

At the end of the planning phase (initiation stage) the steering group approves the risk management approach and the current risk register, containing the risks identified so far and the status of the corresponding measures. In the case of go/no-go decisions (about the transition to a next stage or the approval of changes) the project manager should submit the current status of the risk register for approval and as a basis for decision-making.

Threats and opportunities

Exploiting opportunities (positive risks) can be equally as relevant as mitigating threats (negative risks). Hence risk management should address both.

A project sponsor says...

'The team had done an excellent job. The design stage was completed three weeks earlier than planned and it was a great design. Unfortunately the people who were needed for the construction work could not be made available any sooner, so the project came to a standstill for three weeks. Right away we lost the time that we had gained. This was a real pity because the project had a very tight schedule. Had we defined this opportunity in advance, we could have taken measures to take advantage from it.'

How do you deal with changes?

Over the past decades probably no factor has had more influence on the development of project management than the increase of dynamics in project environments. In a rapidly changing world the occurrence of changes instead of being the exception has become the norm, and basically there are two answers on this. On the one hand, change management has obtained a much more prominent position in the classic waterfall project approaches – that is, approaches based on a sequential development process with phases such as conception, initiation, analysis, design, construction, testing, implementation, production and maintenance. The waterfall approach, however, has a fundamental vulnerability for changes: changes in one of the later phases lead to rework in all the previous phases, so in a highly uncertain and dynamic environment the burden of change management processes and the documentation they require can practically bring a project to a standstill.

This is why in certain sectors (ICT, innovation, product development) the agile approaches have become a popular alternative, based on short stages, each focused on design, realization, testing, implementation and handover to production of part of a solution, trying to achieve quality not through exact specification and control but through direct cooperation between users and specialists who have a mandate to spend a specified amount of time (time-boxing). Unfortunately these approaches are not suitable for all types of project: before you build a bridge you need a complete detailed design.

Waterfall approach

The waterfall approach requires the establishment of a formal change management procedure with the aim to execute those changes that have been approved at the appropriate management level, in a controlled and transparent way. Changes should be approved if they help to realize the project's business case.

The basis for effective and efficient decision-making on changes is: 1) a clear baseline, which is among other things a clear record of the approved version of a specification or deliverable; 2) clearly defined authorities for each management level regarding the approval of changes to this baseline.

The steering group can keep the authority to approve changes entirely for itself. However, if you expect a lot of change requests, consider delegating the authority to approve small changes to a person (named change authority) or board (named change control board) who can approve these change requests within certain budgetary limits per change request and/or per stage. A member of the steering group, for example the senior user, can fulfil the role of change authority or chair the change control board. These roles may also be delegated to the project manager. Elementary for this role is the disposition of a budget for the execution of the changes to be approved, the change budget. The project manager keeps a record of the status of all changes, including the status of decision-making, in a document named change register or issue register. The project manager includes substantial changes in the periodic performance report.

Steering group decision-making

The project manager submits the proposed change management approach to the steering group as a part of the project management plan. It should define the roles and responsibilities, the change control procedures and the way that changes are documented.

The steering group can approve or reject a change request, or decide that the business case of further continuation of the project has become negative and decide to close the project. For adequate decision-making on changes it is essential that the steering group has a change budget.

The steering group may want to bring about a change at its own initiative, but this may be quite risky since no impact analysis will have taken place. In these cases the project manager should prepare this decision as a change request and submit it to the steering group for approval.

A project sponsor says...

A public sector organization was working on a project that would enable citizens to enter data through a website instead of through paper forms. This would make its data entry department obsolete, which, according to the business case, would imply savings of $20 million a year. This equated to almost $100,000 per working day:

'As a project sponsor, I did not have a change budget, all budget increases had to be approved by the board of directors. When the

> project manager came with an urgent change request it took me a week to get their approval. The damage in terms of lost benefits as a result of the delay came to nearly $500,000, while the value of the change request was only $20,000. Obviously, my mandate was not adequate to manage the business case.'

Agile approaches

One could say that the agile approaches are made for dealing with changes. There is no baseline to be approved as a basis for the empowerment of the project manager. Instead a list of prioritized work items is defined (the product backlog), defining requirements for which the project team is to seek a solution. The project team, consisting of user representatives and specialists, in one integrated process designs, creates and tests a solution. All this significantly reduces the amount of documentation to be adapted in the case of changes.

Agile approaches require that the authority to decide on (detailed) functionality of the results is delegated from the steering group to the product owner. As a project sponsor you can exercise control at the start of each stage (called iteration, preferably with a duration of a few weeks) when the previous stage is evaluated and the priorities for the new stage are redefined.

Summary

Risks as well as changes are unavoidable. They provide threats as well as opportunities and, therefore, uncertainty should be embraced instead of avoided. Proper risk management and change control are prerequisites to be successful in a dynamic environment.

When dealing with risk, ensure that the approach (top-down and bottom-up) allows coming to a full understanding of the project-related risk and focus on the proper assignment of responsibilities: risk ownership. Ensure that the project manager keeps the risk register up to date and includes the main risks in their performance reports.

With respect to changes, some types of project allow the choice of a fundamentally more flexible approach, called agile. In a classic waterfall approach, issues to focus on as a project sponsor are a clear definition of the authority to decide on change requests, a clear baseline and adherence to the change control procedures. Ensure that the project manager keeps the change register up to date and includes the main changes in their performance reports.

Note

1 Translated from 'Waarom doen we dit eigenlijk? De businesscase als succesfactor van projecten' ('Why are we doing this? The business case as project success factor') (Van der Molen, 2013).

10 Assessing documents

Project sponsors and steering group members get an overload of documents as a basis for their decision-making. Within this multitude of information it is often hard to find the essential information about the project. This chapter helps you to efficiently assess the four most relevant types of document:

1 The business case document: the answer to the question 'Why are we doing this project?' and the frame of reference for all decision-making.

2 A plan (whether a project plan or a stage plan): the answer to the question 'What are we going to realize, how, when will it be delivered and at what cost?'

3 A performance report (also known as highlight report or monthly report): the answer to the question 'How are things really going, compared to the plan?'

4 A change request: a proposal to change the plan.

For each of these four types of document this chapter contains a checklist. Judge for yourself which questions are relevant for a specific project. Where necessary, get an auditor or other specialist to independently scrutinize a document for you.

How do you assess a business case document?

A proper business case document is suitable for the following:

- to underpin the investment decision;
- to share the relevance of the project with stakeholders;

- as a foundation to assign benefit realization responsibilities;
- as a frame of reference for decisions on project continuation and changes;
- as a basis for the evaluation of project success.

The questions set out in Checklist 10.1 may be asked to assess the quality of a business case document. For more information about the business case, see Chapter 1.

CHECKLIST 10.1 Questions to ask to assess the quality of a business case document

Reasons	What existing corporate strategies or policies are relevant for this project? Is it clear how the project goal is related to these strategies or policies, allowing all stakeholders to understand the relevance of this project for the organization? Has the main reason behind the project been briefly summarized, in a way that can be communicated unambiguously and powerfully (one-liner)? Is it clear what will happen if we don't do the project or don't do it now?
Options	Have several options been discussed and has an argumented choice been made? There are always at least two options, 'do something' and 'do nothing'.
Proposed Benefits	Is it clear what the main benefits are and which ones are just nice to have? Are the benefits measurable? Are the benefits quantified? Is it clear when the benefits are expected to be realized? Have benefit owners been found – that is, persons accepting responsibility to realize them based on the proposed project deliverable? Have disbenefits been defined and quantified, and have they been taken into account in the investment decision?

(*Continued*)

CHECKLIST 10.1 (*Continued*)

Timescale	Is it clear what the critical delivery dates are? Is it clear why these dates are relevant? A desirable delivery date is not the same as a necessary delivery date. A one-day schedule overrun can have just a minor impact, but can also be fatal.
Cost	Have all types of cost been included?: • Direct costs such as costs of purchasing, development, building, switching production, training or implementation. • Overhead costs such as project or programme management and auditing. • Lost income during project execution and/or switching production. • Costs of temporary facilities. • Costs of risk reservations. • Costs of compensation of negative effects and costs of claims. • Permanent costs of exploitation, maintenance, management and licences. Are all suppliers committed to these costs by means of existing price agreements or proposals, or are the costs yet to be agreed?
Risk	Have the main risks been identified? Have their probability and impact been assessed realistically? Have stakeholders with different viewpoints (project sponsor, users, suppliers, specialists, opponents of the project) been involved in the risk assessment? Has the resulting risk assessment been tested by those in the organization who are responsible for risk management?
Investment Analysis	Has, taking into account all previously mentioned aspects, an assessment of the business case been made based on the current corporate standards for investment analysis? Has the resulting investment analysis been assessed by those in the organization who are responsible for investment assessment?
General	Has the business case been assessed by knowledgeable persons who don't have a stake in the project?

How do you assess a plan?

A plan is an agreement with the project manager about what they are going to deliver, with what quality, when and at what cost.[1] It should be suitable for the following:

- To ensure user commitment (are they willing to use the proposed deliverables for the purpose they are made for, and where necessary to contribute to their development?).
- To ensure supplier commitment (are they willing to realize these deliverables under these conditions?).
- As a yardstick to measure performance during project execution.
- To underpin the business case (do these deliverables allow realization of these benefits?).
- As a frame of reference to assess the impact of change requests.

For a steering group the relevant plans are the project plan and, when applicable, stage plans. A project plan contains an outline schedule, an outline cost estimate and a division into management stages. A stage plan is made right before the start of a next stage and defines the exact deliverables, the resources to be deployed and the quality activities to be performed. Project plans and stage plans basically have the same layout. In a simple project there is only one plan: the project plan.

The questions set out in Checklist 10.2 can be asked to assess the quality of a plan.

CHECKLIST 10.2 Questions to ask to assess the quality of a project plan

Preconditions	Is it clear what essential preconditions are required and are you able to fulfil them?
Assumptions	On what assumptions (such as hour rates or number of working weeks lost due to weather conditions) is the plan based and are they realistic?

(Continued)

CHECKLIST 10.2 *(Continued)*

Deliverables	Is the end result of the project described unambiguously as a deliverable or deliverables? Are intermediate results described as deliverables? Is the work breakdown structure (a hierarchical decomposition of the total scope of work) detailed enough to allow frequent and reliable performance measurement? Are the descriptions of deliverables detailed enough for stakeholders to buy in to them? Is it clear who will be the owner of the deliverables? Is the senior user willing to ensure a smooth transfer of these deliverables to operation and maintenance? Is the senior supplier willing to ensure that the deliverables will be realized?
Interfaces and Dependencies	In the case of interfaces with other projects: is our project dependent on another project (which implies a planning risk), or is the other project dependent on our project (which might imply extra time pressure or quality expectations)? In the case of dependencies: are they resource dependencies (our project needs the same resources as another project) or deliverable dependencies (our project will not be able to continue before another project has realized a certain deliverable)? Are all external dependencies explicitly listed? Beware, if X is a deliverable that we do need and that we will not realize ourselves, in a project plan such an external dependency can be hidden in a section named: • points of departure (for example the point of departure that X is present); • preconditions (for example the precondition that X is present); • assumptions (for example the assumption that X is present); • interfaces (for example an interface with a project that is expected to realize X); • exclusions (for example the statement that realizing X is out of scope). Is it clear which parts of our project depend on these external factors? For each dependency on deliverables to be created by others (also called external products): is it clear who is going to create them and when they should ultimately be available?

CHECKLIST 10.2 *(Continued)*

Schedule	Is the work breakdown structure based on a decomposition of deliverables, thus allowing performance measurement to be underpinned by the realization of deliverables? Does the schedule contain enough slack? Is there enough time for rework (the correction of rejected deliverables)? Is it clear what staff and other resources should be made available and when? Has the schedule been assessed independently?
Budget	Is the budget consistent with the decomposition of the deliverables – that is, are all budget items related to one of the deliverables and have all deliverables been included in the budget? Exceptions to this are overhead items such as for project management, project support and project team facilities, which are included in the budget but are not related to deliverables. Is a contingency budget included? Is a change budget included? Is a budget included for incidentals, following from planning uncertainties? Has the budget been assessed independently?
Quality and Quality Control	What quality standards are applicable? Are the quality requirements measurable and related to the deliverables? Are quality activities planned and is it clear who will perform them?
In the Case of a Project Plan: Management Stages	Is there a decomposition into management stages? Is the division of the project into management stages and the timing of the stage transitions in line with the needs of the steering group for strategic decision-making? Are stage transitions related to the realization of relevant deliverables, thus allowing the steering group to get a reliable picture of project performance?
Tolerances	Is it clear what the project manager's mandate is and when they need to raise the alarm? Is this arrangement in line with the project's business case and risks?
Connection with the Business Case	Do the deliverables defined allow the realization of the business case? Are the budget and schedule consistent with the current version of the business case?

How do you assess a performance report?

A performance report (also named status report or highlight report) is a periodical report from the project manager to the project sponsor and the steering group. It should:

- give a clear picture of the project status at the end of the reporting period compared to the baseline (the plan), and make clear if the project manager considers the project to be under control;
- list relevant achievements and issues of the past period and list the forecasted achievements and relevant risks of the period to come;
- be concise and focus on the essentials, but at the same time support ownership and commitment of the steering group members by giving enough details for them to understand their responsibilities.

The precise layout of performance reports should be in line with corporate standards and the project management plan.

A project sponsor says...

'Beware of glossy performance reports. If they look too good, no one dares to question the content.'

The questions in Checklist 10.3 can be asked to assess the quality of a performance report.

Not all questions in Checklist 10.3 always need to have a positive answer. For instance, you might find it acceptable that the data on which a performance report is based are not subject to project assurance and not independently scrutinized. As a project sponsor, however, you should know this and make a deliberate decision to accept it or not. The accountability for the reliability for performance reporting remains yours.

CHECKLIST 10.3   Questions to ask to assess the quality of a performance report

General	Is the reporting format in line with the company standard and the project management plan? Is it clear what reporting period is covered by the report?
Schedule	Is there an objective basis for performance measurement – that is, is it clear what deliverables have been realized, when they were realized and when they should have been realized according to the schedule? For work in progress: have expected delivery dates been estimated and have they been compared with the planned delivery dates in the schedule? Has the impact of all deviations from schedule been translated into an overall impact on the expected completion date of the stage or the project?
Budget	Is there an objective basis for the measurement of financial realization – that is, is it clear what deliverables have actually cost and what they should have cost according to the budget? Have expected costs been estimated for work in progress and have they been compared with the relevant items in the budget?
Quality	Do the quality measurements (quality register) contain entries for each deliverable that has been reported as being completed – and do they show what quality activities have taken place?
Issues	Is it clear what impact the issues (including change requests) will have on time, costs, quality, scope, benefits and risk?
Risks	Is there a clear distinction between issues (facts in the past) and risks (possibilities in the future)? Is each risk analysed in terms of probability and impact on time, costs, quality, scope and benefits?
Forecast	Is there an explicit statement about the project still being in control (more precisely: within the agreed tolerances)? Do the budget and schedule forecasts take into account the impact of issues and risks? In case the performance report contains deviations outside tolerances: were they reported directly when they occurred?
Reliability	Are the data on which the performance report is based subject to project assurance and are they independently scrutinized?

> ### Be careful with percentage complete
>
> Let's presume that an activity is scheduled to last two weeks. At the end of these two weeks, the project manager reports that the activity is 50 per cent complete. What does this mean? Does it mean that:
>
> - The activity was started on time and will take another two weeks to completion.
>
> - The activity was started one week late and will take another week to completion.
>
> - The activity was started on time, has lost a week due to illness, and since no more setbacks are expected will take just one more week to completion.
>
> - The activity was started yesterday, appears to be quite overestimated and will be completed tomorrow.
>
> All these options are valid assumptions. The conclusion is that looking only at the percentage complete is not a valid way to report progress. The project manager should add an estimate of the expected completion date, to be compared with the baseline. The same goes for financial status reporting.

How do you assess a change request?

A change request is a proposal to bring about a change in the baseline of the project, which often requires an additional investment. One could say that a change request is (a miniature version of) a combination of a plan and a business case, since it proposes what to do and why. In the case of a very large change request, use the checklists of the corresponding documents.

When discussing a change request for approval, the questions in Checklist 10.4 may be asked. In order not to burden a steering group meeting too much, consider asking the project manager to inform you before the meeting. A structural way to spare the steering group is to establish a change control board, as discussed in Chapter 5.

CHECKLIST 10.4 Questions to ask when discussing a change
request for approval

Initiator	Who initiated the change request? (This can be relevant information to understand its background.)
Background and Reason	What issue triggered the change request? What problem is it supposed to solve? What other options are there to solve the same problem? Why is this the best solution? How does it support the business case? What happens if we reject this change request?
Scope	What existing project deliverables will be affected? What new or changed deliverables are proposed and are they clearly defined?
Quality	What changes to the existing quality management plan are proposed? What quality activities are needed to test the quality of the proposed new or changed deliverables, and who will perform them?
Schedule	What changes to the existing schedule are proposed?
Budget	What changes to the existing budget are proposed?
Risks	Have the risks of the change request been assessed, and what mitigating measures are proposed?
Benefits and Disbenefits	How does the change request impact the benefits of the project? Does this change request bring about any *dis*benefits? Are these changes accepted by the relevant benefit owners?
Impact on Investment Analysis	What is the impact of the change request on the investment analysis?

Summary

In the multitude of project documents you have to deal with as a project sponsor it is important to focus on the essentials. Check if the business case document is suitable as a basis for go/no-go decisions and decisions on change requests. Check if a plan is suitable as a yardstick to measure project performance. Check if performance reports underpin that the project is under control. In case of change requests, check if they make clear what their impact is on scope, quality, schedule, budget, risk and benefits.

Note

1 This section is not about the management plans, such as the quality management plan or the risk management plan.

Why do projects exceed their budget and what can you do about this?

Experience shows that projects tend to exceed their budget even if this possibility was taken into account when drafting the budget. This chapter lists 10 structural causes of budget overruns and what you can do against this as a project sponsor. Judge for yourself which measures are most relevant for your project.

The first cause is generally applicable when people want something:

- optimism bias.

In addition there are many factors that cause the scope of a project to increase or change during project execution:

- an increase in user insight;
- excessive specialist influence;
- changes in the project environment;
- insufficient project control.

Even when a project's scope is under control, things can still go wrong. The project may still exceed its budget because of:

- blind spots in the schedule;
- technical issues;
- Parkinson's law;

- decision-making delays;
- suppliers forcing up prices.

Optimism bias

In the global best-seller *Thinking, Fast and Slow* (Kahnemann, 2011), based on extensive research, the author shows how facts that confirm our assumptions are found by us to be more relevant than other facts, and how we overrate the reliability of our estimates, even when again and again the facts prove the opposite. It is the basis of a structural optimism bias.

In practice, this natural bias is further strengthened by the interests that are related to projects. When people really want a project, they need support from others and in order to gain this support they need arguments. As a consequence it is in the interest of the proponents of a project to have the most positive business case and to confirm each other's positive expectations. People who see risks readily are labelled as troublemakers. The result is an overestimate of the benefits and an underestimate of the risks, the costs and the time needed.

Of all the causes of project overruns, optimism bias is probably the most difficult to overcome. An extensive overview of factors leading

Major interests

Especially in the case of large infrastructure projects in the public domain (bridges, tunnels, underground connections) large interests are at stake when creating public and political support. Based on research into infrastructure megaprojects Bent Flyvbjerg reports systematic overestimation of transport requirements and systematic underrating of risks (Flyvbjerg *et al*, 2003). The project sponsors themselves are part of this game as soon as they have expressed support for a particular project. Starting with an overoptimistic estimate and then applying for additional resources during execution is sometimes a deliberate strategy to get a project through the decision-making process, thus creating a fait accompli for a parliament or city council.

to a structural overestimate of the benefits of projects can be found in *Managing Benefits* (Jenner, 2012).

If you have an interest in a realistic business case, get it checked by specialists who do not have a stake in the project; let opponents of the project come forward with arguments and seriously investigate them. Scrutinize the assumptions that lie at the basis of the calculation of benefits and check if any disbenefits, costs and risks have possibly been overlooked.

Increase in user insight

It might be hard for users to have a clear picture of the end result in advance and to be aware of what impact this result will have. During the execution of the project they gain more understanding of their own needs and of the possibilities to satisfy them. Depending on the type of project, it might even be inevitable for this to happen. New requirements may arise from a serious need not addressed before, but may also be just nice to have. To make sure that things do not run out of hand, take preventive measures:

- Although an increase in user insight is a very common cause of exceeding the budget, it is not often included in risk analyses. Make sure this cause is listed as a risk and that mitigating actions are defined. These can vary from inserting a prototyping stage to establishing a more rigid change control procedure.

- Be sure to involve users in the project as early as possible, in order to initiate their thinking and learning process as soon as possible.

- A clear business case is a good framework within which to assess change requests. Make sure it is properly used.

- Do not allow committees exclusively made up of users to make decisions about changes, unless under strict conditions. Make sure that the user representation does not have a numerical superiority on the steering group. It should be ensured that, when weighing up costs against functionality, giving priority to cost is a valid option. When weighing up contradictory functional user demands, the project sponsor's interest comes before the (sometimes costly) satisfaction of all users.

- Consider freezing specifications and refusing to consider change requests before the project is completed.

- The reverse approach is deliberately not to define detailed specifications but to fix the budget and to make the scope dependent on what is feasible within this budget. This is where agile project approaches are suitable.

- Restrict the size of projects (consider splitting up large projects into smaller ones) and celebrate the success of each independently and successfully completed project.

Excessive specialist influence

A professional with an overly zealous attitude may love to spend extra time developing an even better solution for users. This specialist is energized by maximizing user satisfaction. This is a variation on scope creep, namely something that could be called quality creep. From the project sponsor's point of view, this excessive specialist involvement provides input with the wrong focus. The zealous attitude is more in the interests of the user than in the interests of the project sponsor. Indeed, if it was in the interests of the project sponsor, it would lead to another balance between cost and quality: to an optimum user satisfaction (based on a proper trade-off against business interests) instead of a maximum user satisfaction.

This focus of specialists on user interest (or their own perception of it) is understandable as a specialist often receives direct recognition and/or disapproval from the users rather than from the project sponsor. Many specialists work on a project without ever meeting the project sponsor.

Preventive measures are:

- First and foremost it is the project manager's responsibility to keep specialists in line and let them know that good is good enough. However, your position as project sponsor allows you to make a difference. By directly clarifying the business case to them, you enable specialists, instead of only aligning themselves to the interests of the user, to also align themselves to the interests of the project sponsor – who from their point of view is often more remote.

- Demand a clear quality plan that lists the acceptance criteria for the deliverables to be realized as well as who is qualified to test them. Get an auditor to check that the quality plan is adhered to.

Changes in the project environment

The project environment, for instance the market, technology or organization, can change during the execution of the project. Consequently the project plan and the way it is executed may have to be adjusted. Whether this leads to a smaller or larger project scope, since part of the original plan has already been executed, this will often imply that work has been done in vain and the total project costs will rise.

Preventive measures are:

- Whenever possible, split up a large, complex project into a number of short simple projects.

- See to it that a project approach is chosen that allows flexibility. For instance, in the case of a project for urban development, decisions about the division of housing types and the level of craftsmanship can be taken as late as possible. In the ICT world, as an alternative to the classical waterfall approach (first complete the design, then complete the realization, and then implement), agile approaches have become popular (see Appendix 3).

- Risk management can mitigate the negative effects of dynamics through preventive or corrective measures. Get members of the steering group to contribute to risk management since they, more than others, have an overview of the project environment and hence are better able to quickly respond to risk. The quicker the response, the less work done in vain and the less the schedule and budget overruns as a consequence.

Insufficient project control

When the adjustment of the project scope to growing insight and changes in the environment becomes a drifting process, the actual scope will get further and further removed from the agreed specifications and the business case. The project may be guided by the issues of the day instead of by the business case – and may gradually get out of control.

Preventive measures are:

- Ensure that the project manager presents a clear baseline to the steering group for approval at the start, including deliverables, schedule, budget and assumptions, which will serve as the framework for the project manager's reports. When necessary, get this baseline detailed for each successive stage in the stage plans. The project manager can then compare their achievements with this baseline in each performance report.

- In case of change requests get the project manager to report their impact in terms of expected deviations from this baseline (in terms of time, money, scope, quality, risk, benefits) so that they can be the subject of explicit decision-making.

- Delegate a project assurance role to check – in between steering group meetings – whether the agreed change control procedure has been used, whether reports are correct and whether recorded (interim) results are in line with the baseline.

Blind spots in the schedule

A common cause, and a very human one for that matter, is that in the planning stage of a complex project some aspects are simply overlooked. Thus the real project scope ends up being larger than expected and this only comes to light during project execution.

Preventing blind spots in plans is primarily the project manager's responsibility. But, at the end of the day, you will be accountable. To check the completeness of a plan, ask several types of question:

- How was the planning process approached? Have all those who could have made a relevant contribution to the planning process participated? When drawing up estimates and schedules, it is useful to have the same work done independently by several people and to compare the results. Once the participants have pointed out their differences and have filled in the gaps in each other's thinking, the process can be repeated. Planning workshops have proven to be a powerful tool in achieving better quality of plans.[1]

- Is the end deliverable accurately described? Does the description include its acceptance criteria as well as who is to test them? Does the same apply to the relevant subdeliverables? Are all activities related to deliverables and are all deliverables related to the end deliverable?

- Did the senior user confirm that the proposed deliverables will allow them to realize the expected benefits?

- Have cost estimates of subprojects been confirmed by the team managers or (sub)contractors who will be responsible for the execution of these subprojects?

- Has the total cost estimate been evaluated against previously executed projects of a similar size and nature? To what conclusion did this lead?

In real life you cannot take away all blind spots. In the end these are usually expressed in the budget as incidentals. Get the project manager to split up the incidentals into the following cost categories in order to keep spending under control:

- contingency budget: for disaster mitigation;

- change budget: for additional costs due to changes in requirements;

- budget for planning uncertainties: for the impact of incorrect scope estimates, setbacks and blind spots in the plan.

The first two points in the above list may be kept as a management reserve for the steering group. The last point is often included in the project manager's budget.

Technical issues

Technical issues are issues arising from the technology not behaving in the way that the specialists had expected it to behave. The risk of these issues is especially high in the case of unproven technology or proven technology applied in a new area. A very tedious aspect of these issues is that, as long as specialists haven't solved them, it is often very hard to say how long they will last and what their impact will be.

Preventive measures are:

- As a project sponsor, from a perspective of risk reduction, you should have a strong preference for the use of proven technology, unless new technology is essential to realize the business case.

- An independent audit can confirm the technical feasibility of the project.

- If there is a technological risk, a proof of concept to be held at the start of the project before the real investments are made can mitigate this risk.

- A fallback scenario (plan B) based on proven technology can help to reduce the impact of technological issues. However, if an acceptable plan B based on proven technology is possible, then why not make this plan A?

Parkinson's law

One of the causes of budget overruns is inherent to the way that a schedule is structured and executed. First there is the schedule's structure. In general, it is impossible to predefine the size of an activity exactly. An estimate is sometimes too high and sometimes too low. A good total project estimate is therefore a combination of too high and too low estimates. During project execution this causes problems. To activities estimated too high the well-known Parkinson's law applies: people tend to fully use up their estimated duration (Parkinson, 1958). Unfortunately, no reverse mechanism applies to activities estimated too low: they will exceed their estimated duration. The result of both is a project exceeding its schedule. I call this Parkinson's law for projects.

> **Parkinson's law for projects**
>
> 'The sum of underestimated activities and overestimated activities is an underestimated project.'

This brings us to the unpleasant conclusion that almost all projects are underestimated, and this conclusion seems to be confirmed by experience. When, for example, an organization finds that, on average, their projects exceed their budgets by 20 per cent, and thus accordingly add 20 per cent to the budget of their next project, most likely this will not entirely solve the problem and this next project will still exceed its budget.

One can try to counter Parkinson's law with technical measures. For example, all activities could be deliberately planned too tight and a corresponding amount of play could be maintained at the discretion of the project manager (Goldratt, 1997). The disadvantage of this approach is that the members of the project team will soon see through it and simply view the schedule as unrealistic, with a negative impact on motivation. I believe that there are no technical or methodological solutions for Parkinson's law, and the only alternative is to take away the drivers behind this behaviour as much as possible:

- All project team members should not only feel committed to their own activities, but also to the overall goal of the project and the customer organization. This has to do with motivation, commitment and organizational culture. A project sponsor can contribute to this by directly sharing the business case with all project team members and answering their questions. Direct contact with the business case owner, and being called to account for their own contribution to the corporate objectives, does have a motivating effect on project team members. This is definitely a lot more motivating than being driven by a team leader at a task level without understanding exactly why. As a project sponsor, if you spend 15 minutes discussing the business case on a project team kick-off meeting, this may be the best 15 minutes spent on the project.

- Stimulate the project manager's entrepreneurship. Getting the project manager and their team to take full responsibility for the project stage as a whole is a prerequisite for this. It might sound contradictory, but empowering the project manager contributes to the solution. Indeed, this provides them with the authority to take corrective action, they can react quickly and are assessed on the basis of the end result. Coming in under budget should of course be assessed more positively than simply achieving the budget. Here lies an important responsibility for the project manager's superior, who will need to let the opinion of the project sponsor have a relevant impact on their own appraisal of the project manager's performance. In the case of an overestimated activity, the project manager will thus be challenged not to use the whole budget. They will not have to return the hours saved on an activity estimated too high to the project sponsor – this would destroy the challenge – but are empowered to use these hours to create some contingency and offset activities that have exceeded their estimate in the same stage. The project manager should publicly praise project team members who perform a task in less time than planned – and explain why this is not a luxury but an absolute necessity in order that the team meets the schedule.

- A resource manager and/or hierarchical manager who is responsible for the appraisal of an employee assigned to a project as a team member can make a relevant contribution to overcoming Parkinson's law. It is very important to include the project manager's opinion of the project team member in the employee's assessment and to tell the employee in advance that this will be done. As a result of this, the relationship between the project manager and the project team member will become less non-committal. In addition, it is important to appraise the employee not only on the basis of their own performance in the project: by including the project result as a whole in the project team member's appraisal, the employee's identification with the project's objectives can be furthered. An employee who is working on an activity with too high an estimate is thus encouraged to let the project manager know that there is time available.

Decision-making delays

Slow decision-making seems an intangible phenomenon: 'If we haven't reached a decision, we simply haven't reached a decision.' Lack of support for the business case or lack of user involvement can result in resistance. Decision-making coming to a standstill can have consequences that drastically affect project performance, such as costly waiting times, decreasing stakeholder support and a downturn in the motivation of the project team.

Preventive measures are:

- Involve stakeholders in the development of the business case, its quantification and its assessment against corporate objectives. This can prevent an ongoing discussion about the relevance of the project and its priorities during project execution. Should this lead to the conclusion that there is not enough justification or support for the project, it is obviously better that this becomes apparent from the outset.

- To avoid resistance during execution or implementation, try to involve as early as possible in the specification of the deliverables those users who can be expected to be opposed to the project.

- Calculate the cost of decision-making delays. Take into account the loss of benefits caused by postponement of the handover of the project deliverable to the operational environment, the cost of project team members and other resources being idle and the loss of credibility of the steering group, all of which may have a negative impact on stakeholder support and project team motivation. Ensure that all steering group members are aware of these costs.

- At the beginning of the project demand that you get the mandate needed to make the necessary decisions in case of changing circumstances.

> ### Leadership
>
> It is perhaps needless to point out that a lot will depend on the role of the project sponsor and, when needed, on their leadership when enforcing decision-making discipline.

Suppliers forcing up prices

A final cause of budget overruns is the dependence on one or more suppliers. Such a dependence can originate in an existing customer–supplier relationship when the changeover to another supplier is too costly (for example, because of technological differences or because of the supplier's customer-specific knowledge). When offering additional services the supplier can then effectively take a monopoly position. Another example is that of contractors who force up prices through the formation of a cartel, thereby preventing the customer organization from contracting work at a reasonable price. Solutions to this problem can mostly be found in the areas of contracting strategy, supplier management and contract management, but they lie outside the scope of this book.

Summary

This chapter discussed structural causes of cost overruns in projects and how to prevent them. Some of the most relevant points of advice in this chapter (not all advice is relevant for all projects) are:

- Get the business case document checked by specialists who do not have a stake in the project, scrutinize the assumptions that lie at the basis of the calculation of benefits and check if any disbenefits, costs or risks have been overlooked.

- Be sure to involve users in the project as early as possible, in order to initiate their thinking and learning process as soon as possible.

- Restrict the size of projects (consider splitting large projects into smaller ones) and celebrate the success of each independently and successfully completed project.

- Ensure that the suppliers and specialists involved understand your business case.

- To allow flexibility, make decisions on details as late as possible and when possible consider an agile approach (see Appendix 3).

- In case of change requests ask the project manager to report their impact in terms of expected deviations from the baseline (time, money, scope, quality, risk, benefits) so that they can be the subject of explicit decision-making.

- Check if the senior user has confirmed that the proposed deliverables will allow them to realize the expected benefits and if cost estimates have been confirmed by the team managers or (sub)contractors.

- Insist on proven technology, unless new technology is essential to realize the business case.

- Stimulate the project manager's entrepreneurship and the engagement of project team members with the business case.

- Calculate the cost of decision-making delays and ensure that all steering group members are aware of these costs.

Note

1 If considering participating in a workshop yourself, you should weigh the advantages of direct participation against the disadvantage of being less impartial when the time comes for you to assess the quality of the resulting plan.

Summary of Part 2

Part 2 discussed a large number of practical issues that any project sponsor has to deal with. Some of the most relevant points of advice are:

- Link the responsibilities of steering group members as closely as possible to their existing accountabilities in the line organization and don't allow people to participate in steering groups without specific individual responsibilities (no free rides).

- Define clear authorities for the project manager in order to enable them to take corrective action effectively.

- In order to come to a reliable insight into the project benefits and to realize them, work closely with the project's stakeholders and organize benefit ownership.

- As a sponsor, in order to achieve quality, to manage risk and to control changes, focus on the proper assignment of business responsibilities.

- Get the business case document checked by specialists who do not have a stake in the project, scrutinize the assumptions that lie at the basis of the calculation of benefits, and check if any disbenefits, costs or risks have been overlooked.

- Consider splitting large projects into smaller ones.

- Be sure to involve users in the project as early as possible, in order to initiate their thinking and learning process as soon as possible.

- Ensure that suppliers and specialists involved understand your business case.

- Insist on proven technology, unless new technology is essential to realize the business case.

PART THREE
Advancing project sponsorship in organizations

Introduction
to Part 3

Advancing project sponsorship in an organization is a change
programme in its own right. In this part of the book, Chapter
12 discusses the challenge: what makes it so difficult? Chapter 13
presents an outline approach, based on my experience over the
past 12 years. Chapter 14 sketches an outline of the most relevant
types of training course and workshop that can be part of a project
sponsorship advancement programme.

Contrary to Part 1 and Part 2, written primarily for the individual
project sponsor, Part 3 is written for individuals involved in the direction, management or execution of project sponsorship advancement
programmes, such as business managers in a role as sponsor or steering group member of such a programme, heads of project management offices, project professionals and management trainers.

The challenge

12

The poor development of project sponsorship in many organizations is often closely linked to the way that managers are educated and rewarded, the way organizations are shaped, the way the project management profession approaches projects, and the behaviour of suppliers. This chapter discusses the main issues in order to come to a proper understanding of the challenge to advance this role.

Conflicting interests

Managers who on the one hand are responsible for the operational management of part of the line organization – such as a team, department or division – on the other hand become responsible for the direction of one or more projects that cross the borderline with other teams, departments or divisions. Operational management often requires direct attention, and management decisions have a direct impact on vital matters such as service delivery, customer satisfaction, employee satisfaction and turnover. The impact of decisions on project direction, however, may take a long time to be noticed. This is a fundamental conflict between short-term and long-term interests. When the pressure is high, it is only natural that the short-term interests of operational management prevail over the long-term interests of realizing the business case of a project. The effect is that a manager reads a report about current customer complaints instead of preparing the next day's steering group meeting, or decides to skip a steering group meeting because they have to solve an urgent operational issue.

Lower status of project management

In some organizations project management has a lower status than line management. Indications may be that project managers earn less than line managers, that superfluous or failing line managers are given charge of a project, or that line managers switching to project management do not receive any additional training. Apparently, in spite of the high failure rate of projects, project management is seen as easier than line management. Or is it just the classic notion that real management is hierarchic? Anyhow, in such an environment the message is clear: if you want a management career, stay away from projects – high risk, low rewards. This does not help to interest line managers in building up project-related capabilities and experience. Instead it stimulates them *not* to engage in projects and to leave them to the project manager as much as possible.

Performance measurement

For sustainable success an organization needs to be good at two kinds of quality (see Chapter 8): *static quality* (to comply with pre-defined requirements with repeating processes and to be predictable – this is what line organizations are made for); and *dynamic quality* (to use creativity to establish something new, a unique result – what project organizations are meant for). Although in different industries there will be another balance between the two, in general it is hard to say which type of quality is more relevant: they are simply both indispensable.

In many organizations, however, most of the parameters used to measure management performance refer to static quality – that is, the direct results of the line organization. As a consequence, managers' participation in projects, and therefore in project steering groups, do not reflect positively on their career prospects. The company's performance management system – with a direct impact on managers' income and career perspectives – tells them that their other duties, related to the management of the line organization, are far more relevant.

Another contradiction is that performance measurement is often related to the separate functions of an organization (such as sales, logistics, marketing), while projects are often cross-functional. If, for example, at an insurance company aiming to increase profitability, a project's business case requires that the most unprofitable customers are let go, it might encounter opposition from the sales managers who are used to getting turnover-related bonuses (Spitzer, 2007).

If you want business managers to participate in steering groups with a positive mindset and strings attached, establishing an adequate performance measurement system is often one of the main challenges.

'The project manager is accountable'

There is a deeply rooted idea that the project manager is accountable for the success of a project. But how can there ever be anything in an organization for which line management is not accountable? When something goes wrong, whether it is fraud, environmental scandals, failing projects or whatever, 'I didn't know' or 'I didn't do it, it was the project manager' is not an acceptable excuse. And indeed it is a line manager, the project sponsor, who assigns or accepts the project manager, makes available the budget, approves the project plan and other documents, accepts the risk and quality measures, approves the change requests and so forth, and ultimately discharges the project manager. The project sponsor thus makes themselves fully responsible for project success, not only for its business result (achieving the business case) but also for its direct project result (ensuring the required deliverables are realized within time and budget). The idea that the project manager is accountable for project success is based on not seeing a project in its full context and, as such, is a limited way of viewing project success.

On top of that, the way we view project management has changed. In the present ever more dynamic world, we have come to realize that it is often impossible to predict what we will need at the end of the project. Changes have become the rule instead of the exceptions to be avoided. The project success no longer depends on the project manager's ability to avoid changes and stick to the plan, but on our ability to benefit from them in order to optimize the project outcome – its contribution to our strategic interests as defined in the business case. For this, the role of business management has become increasingly relevant.

The idea – or rather the illusion – that the project manager is accountable for the success of the project is nevertheless firmly in place. Replacing this idea with a balanced view on the project manager's, project sponsor's and steering group member's responsibilities and accountabilities is one of the main challenges of advancing project sponsorship in organizations. This can meet severe resistance: sticking to the illusion of only the project manager being responsible may feel comfortable for some business managers, and in some corporate cultures it is a taboo to suggest that business managers should be held accountable for project success. Equally there can be severe resistance against this idea among project managers who see it as a threat to the relevance of their profession. Overcoming this obsolete idea is crucial for improving project performance in organizations.

Business schools

In the many years that I've been working with business managers I have hardly met anyone who had received training to prepare them for the role of project sponsor. The universities and business schools that were responsible for their education were mostly focused on business operations as well as high-level business change, but did not prepare them for a role as sponsor of an 'everyday' project. Many of these schools do offer a project management overview, but that is like offering a summary of the training for mechanics to someone who needs driving lessons. In short, project sponsorship falls in a gap: the world of business management education considers everything related to projects as project management, and the project management world unfortunately is fully focused on the role of the project manager and hardly supports the roles of the project sponsor and steering group members, thus leaving it to each business manager to reinvent the wheel of project sponsorship.

Project management literature

Most project management books look at projects through the eyes of the project manager. They tell the project manager what to do at each stage of the project and how to do it. All other persons involved – customers, suppliers, business managers, team members – are 'others', called stakeholders, and as such are subject to stakeholder management. This implies that even the project sponsor is a stakeholder to be managed by the project manager, the latter thus implicitly behaving as if they are the owner of the project. I say that this turns the world upside down, because obviously the project sponsor is the owner of the project and should direct the project manager. But in the multitude of project management books written from the project manager's perspective you cannot find how to do this, thus again leaving business managers without support for their involvement in projects.

Professional organizations

In line with the limitations of existing project management literature, professional organizations that claim to develop project management expertise, in reality focus on one role in the project management process, namely the role of the project manager. In addition they have a natural tendency to promote the profession – in many organizations project managers have a lower status than business managers, so indeed they have a case. This again confirms the idea that a good project manager is the solution for all project problems instead of meeting the challenge to have business managers to accept responsibility for their projects.

Suppliers

Some suppliers of project management services claim that hiring their project managers is a guarantee for success. Not only does this come from a rather narrow perception of project success (as discussed in the Introduction of this book), it confirms the aforementioned illusion about the project manager being responsible and the project sponsor role apparently being irrelevant. It takes courage for a supplier to make clear that project success also depends on the quality of project sponsorship.

Project managers

In the absence of real ownership on the business side, many project managers have learned to play a complementary role and to act as if they own the project themselves. This is what in transactional analysis is called a game: if one person takes over the responsibility of another person, they confirm the other person in their behaviour of not taking responsibility (Berne, 1964). For project managers, one of the main challenges is to avoid/stop this game – that is, to break this circle of confirming each other's behaviour, without of course unacceptably harming their projects.

This situation, of project managers taking over aspects of project ownership, is reflected in the way that project managers work and in how the project management profession has developed, focusing on the project manager as virtual owner and reducing all other stakeholders, including the project sponsor, to stakeholders to be managed. It is common for project managers to have a strong emphasis on *making the project manageable and controllable for themselves* and to pay little attention to *making the project transparent and easy to direct for the project sponsor and their steering group*. Some project management methods don't give any support to how the project manager can facilitate the project sponsor in directing the project, including aspects such as maintenance of the business case, clearly defining their own mandate as a project manager or preparing steering group decision-making. Enrichment of the professional tooling and role perception of project managers will be needed in order to facilitate business managers to fully fulfil project sponsor roles.

Summary

In most organizations just holding training sessions for business managers is not enough to bring about a relevant change towards successful project sponsorship. The real challenge is to overcome deeply rooted views on the roles of business managers and project managers, and the influence of existing performance measurement systems and other environmental factors that are often not in support of successful project sponsorship.

13

The approach

In my view there can be no standard approach for advancing project sponsorship in organizations. Given the many dependencies, some of which are listed in Chapter 12, the point of departure for such a change programme is unique for every organization. And it will not be conducted in isolation, since there will be more challenges in the area of organizational development that focus on the same target groups. Therefore in this chapter I present some considerations to help you to come to a tailor-made approach, including the trade-off between a top-down and a bottom-up approach, the role of several target groups, how to align with the existing context, how to integrate with leadership and management development, and in the context of relationships with performance measurement and benefit management.

Align with existing context

If an initiative aiming to improve project sponsorship is completely alien to anything else going on in an organization, it is hard to imagine that it will encounter much support. A business case should explain why the initiative is started, what advantages you expect (the summary to Part 1 might offer inspiration) and how they contribute to corporate strategy in a way that everyone can understand. And indeed, as I said in Chapter 1, 'a clear business case fits on a beer mat'.

This requires that the focus of the initiative and the way it is presented is adapted to its context. For instance:

- In an organization with a strong focus on management development, where leadership is a key theme, you might connect the advancement of project sponsorship with leadership development.

- In an organization with a strong focus on individual accountability, you might emphasize that the four principles of successful project sponsorship help project sponsors to achieve more with less effort.

Make life easier

It was 15 minutes after the due commencement time before all the participants of the project sponsorship training course were present. The group consisted of product managers and marketing managers from an insurance company. For most of them their body language – leaning back, not concentrated – expressed that they would rather be somewhere else. When I asked as part of the introductions what was their motivation for attending the course, some of them simply admitted: 'We are here because we were told to be here.' Indeed the company's marketing director had decided that all her subordinates had to undertake the training on a mandatory basis.

I showed my understanding for their position: marketing and product managers should have their main focus on the outside world, and it's only natural that they want to spend as little time as possible on projects. I then explained that this was precisely why the training was called 'more strategic control *for less effort*' and why the whole content was in line with this title, precisely to help them keep their hands free for their primary responsibility. I invited them to closely monitor the content of the training: 'If we discuss anything here today that does not help you to gain more strategic control *with less effort*, then please interrupt me, because that would mean that I am trying to teach you something that you will never put into practice.'

This is precisely what they did. Before the first coffee break all participants sat upright, because they felt that what was discussed was not another burden on top of their existing duties, but something that would help them to make life easier and more successful.

Another way to align with the existing context lies in the way that you engage the participants of a training course. Ask the participants (before the training or at the start of the training) what obstructions they encounter when trying to make a success of their project and put the answers on a sheet on the wall. Refer to these throughout the training and when evaluating the training at the end, thus helping the participants to connect the content of the training with what they experience in daily life. In addition, encourage them to bring in cases from their own practice.

Tip for the PRINCE2 environment

When implementing PRINCE2 in an organization it is best to include project sponsorship training courses as early as possible. Business managers often have a strong reluctance against an overload of project methodology, and their participation in the change process helps to find a proper balance between pragmatism and professionalism. This enables you to establish project governance first, as a condition for a tailored implementation of PRINCE2.

Start where the momentum is

Theoretically it seems ideal to work top-down, to work with the board of directors and create a vision and a business case for the advancement of project sponsorship, train the business managers and so forth. In real life it often doesn't work this way: you will need to work carefully to organize ownership for the initiative step by step.

An initiative to improve project sponsorship often comes from a single member of the board of directors who still has to gain support from their colleagues, from a head of a project management office, a manager in project management or a portfolio manager. Without an accepted vision and business case for the advancement of project sponsorship, they want to make a start by training a first group of project sponsors, hoping that they will be enthusiastic and become ambassadors for the initiative. This has an obvious advantage: because participation to the training sessions is voluntary, there are only motivated participants, which is an ideal condition for successful training. The added value reported by the participants will confirm the effect of the training and help to further increase the momentum. This way the initiative spreads like an oil stain.

In my practice, successful initiatives for the advancement of project sponsorship in an organization were often based on a hybrid approach. They started with a pilot (a project sponsorship training or a steering group start-up session: for details see Chapter 14 'Tips for training courses and workshops'), following the oil-stain approach. After proven success they were taken over by senior management, improving the conditions for successful project sponsorship and deciding that the remaining members of the target group should also be involved.

Include all target groups

A project sponsorship change programme should include the following target groups:

- The board of directors, to help them investigate to what extent existing performance measurement, and elements of corporate culture connected to it, drives business managers to find their operational responsibilities more important than their project responsibilities – and how to change it.

- Project sponsors and other business managers taking part in steering groups, to help them come to a full understanding of project success, rethink the conviction that project managers are responsible for it, and to take responsibility for their projects using the four principles presented in this book.

- Project managers, to help them understand how their taking ownership of the project can confirm their project sponsor in not taking ownership – and how to stop this; to develop skills to improve the project sponsor's comfort by bringing more transparency into their project and making it easier to give strategic direction.

- Project auditors, to help them see that some driving factors of project success do not lie in the proper application of a project management method by the project manager, but in business management accepting its responsibilities and acting accordingly.

- Project controllers, to help them broaden their attention from costs towards benefits and from financial to non-financial achievements, and to become a true sparring partner of the project sponsor when it comes to understanding the drivers of project success.

Address several levels of personal change

Achievements are just the tip of the iceberg of personal change. Achievements depend on behaviour, most of which you don't see because you are not always around. Behaviour is influenced by knowledge, but knowledge itself is not enough if the person in question does not have the competences to use it. That is why a transfer of knowledge often does not lead to a change in behaviour. And that is why in a project sponsorship training, the participants should not only learn about the four principles of project sponsorship success, but also practise their application in their own projects. But even then, if a business manager possesses the right competences but holds the conviction that the project manager is responsible for project success, it is likely that under pressure they will give priority to their other duties and leave the project to the project manager. Therefore, project sponsorship training should also address convictions. Instead of instruction-oriented training this requires experience-based learning, a highly interactive approach based on one's own experiences (Kolb, 2015).

In many environments even this is not enough. If existing performance measurement and reward systems effectively incentivize managers to give priority to their operational duties rather than their project-related duties (see Chapter 12), there is a good chance that you still get the behaviour that you measure and reward, with failing project sponsorship as a result. In most environments it is the board of directors who can most effectively influence this, by sharing clear values related to project-oriented behaviour of business managers ('a good business manager in our company takes responsibility for their projects') and by adapting performance measurement and reward systems in order to reflect that change is just as important as operations.

Performance measurement

Incorporating the right incentives into an organization's performance measurement and reward systems does not guarantee that all people will behave the way they should, because not everyone's behaviour is equally driven by these incentives – there are other factors that influence behaviour. Applying the wrong incentives, however, does guarantee that at least some of the people will not behave the way they should, because some people have their behaviour fully driven by formal incentives.

This is why, when creating a positive environment for successful project sponsorship, one should pay very careful attention to the impact of the organization's performance measurement and reward systems, but without expecting that this will be enough.

In addition to the above, the ever more complex environments of organizational change make increasing demands on soft skills in general, which is an extra reason to consider integrating project sponsorship training in a broader management development programme.

Improve benefit management

In general, project governance (at corporate level, focused on the project portfolio), project direction (by the project sponsor, directing an individual project) and project management should be focused on creating value for the organization and its stakeholders. Although the benefits of change should outweigh the costs, in many organizations there is more attention given to cost management than to benefit management. Consider holding additional training in the area of benefit management. The basics of benefit management are relevant for the board of directors, project sponsors, line managers involved in projects, HR managers, controllers, auditors, strategy consultants, and change professionals such as project managers. See Chapter 7 for an overview of business management responsibilities regarding benefit management.

Practise what you preach

If change is all about creating added value, this also goes for project sponsorship training. Practise what you preach, and measure the effect of your training activities two or three months after each training session. Hold a brief enquiry among participants with the following questions:

- Which parts of the training did you apply in practice?
- What added value did this deliver for your project or the organization?
- What suggestions do you have to increase the added value of the training?
- What obstructions do you encounter to apply (parts of) the training content in your own organization?
- What suggestions do you have to remove these obstructions?

If certain elements of the training content are not mentioned by the participants, consider removing them or radically changing them. See if you can strengthen the parts that are reported to have added value. This way, the training will get stronger and stronger. The answers to the last two questions are relevant input for further organizational development.

Work with authoritative trainers

Given the enormous challenge of advancing project sponsorship, trainers who work with business managers should comply with high standards. They should:

- Have experience as a business manager with responsibility for projects and hence have experienced the dilemma of making time for project direction while being under pressure to deliver short-term operational achievements (for a project manager who does not share this experience this all seems too easy, which makes them less convincing as a trainer for business managers).

- Have experience as a management trainer, understand that training is not about transferring knowledge but about helping people to change behaviour, and be able to address the convictions, values and interests that drive behaviour.

- Be knowledgeable in the areas of change management, project and programme management, business case management, benefit management and portfolio management.

- Be independent from supplier interests in order to be convincing when discussing steering group composition, business cases,[1] contract issues and other potential areas of conflict between project sponsor and supplier.

Continuous effort

Advancing project sponsorship in an organization is not a temporary endeavour, it requires continuous effort. Once you have defined a best practice for project sponsorship in your organization, consider integrating it in the quality system. Once you have developed an approach for training business managers and other target groups, integrate it in the organization's management development programme. If steering group start-up meetings appear to be successful, make sure that the budget for such meetings become an accepted part of project budgets. If key performance indicators and management contracts have been adapted to the requirements of successful project sponsorship, see to it that in future years the same considerations are taken into account.

Summary

Advancing project sponsorship in an organization requires an approach focused on all groups involved: the board of directors; the project sponsors and other business managers taking part in steering groups; the project managers; the project auditors; and the project controllers. It should be based on a critical evaluation of existing performance management systems and, where possible, align with existing management development programmes and change initiatives. It should not be focused merely on the transfer of knowledge but address several levels of personal change in order to achieve a change in behaviour. Advancing project sponsorship, instead of being a temporary endeavour, will require a permanent effort.

Note

1   It is in the interest of a sponsoring organization that a business case is as realistic as possible and helps to optimize the return on investment. It is in the interest of a supplier that a business case is as positive as possible and helps to maximize the investment.

Tips for training courses and workshops

14

A change programme aiming to advance project sponsorship requires, like any other change programme, all kinds of interventions. A significant part of these interventions will consist of training courses and workshops. This chapter defines the proposed results of the most relevant types of training course or workshop, presuming that you work with experienced trainers who have the general capabilities needed to prepare and lead them. When actually preparing training courses or workshops, you will always need to adapt the approach and content to the starting situation and goals of your organization and the level of motivation and competence of the participants.

Training the board of directors

Although for a board of directors changing the business may be even more important than running the business, they will seldom take the time to reflect on how to create the conditions for successful projects. So be happy if they take half a day, and focus on the essence of this.

The basic insight to achieve is that the accountability for project success does not end with the project sponsors. The final accountability lies with the board of directors and the behaviour of the board of directors has a decisive influence on the achievements of the business managers of their organization in their roles as project sponsors.

The creation of the conditions for successful project sponsorship requires that the board of directors clearly understands, communicates and acts according to the following statements:

- A project is only successful if the business goal is achieved.
- Line management is accountable for the success of projects.
- For a specific project, the project sponsor is the one who represents line management.

Acting in line with these statements implies a critical examination of the existing performance management system, including key performance indicators, management contracts and the reward system based on them. Discussing the essence of benefit management can offer insights that help to integrate strategy development, portfolio management, change management, performance management and accounting by providing a common language and a binding approach to all these areas of expertise that in the end should contribute to the same goal – that is, realizing corporate strategy.

While some boards of directors are very hands on, others are content to be more strategic. In case the members of the board of directors perform project sponsor roles for the most strategic projects themselves, discuss the principles of successful project sponsorship presented in this book. Focus on the first two principles, *share the business case* and *organize ownership*, which are the most relevant ones for giving strategic direction.

Training the project sponsors and steering group members

When training business managers who perform roles as project sponsors or steering group members, the main challenge is often to bring about a change of attitude and conviction. Instead of thinking that project managers are responsible for project success, it is essential that business managers accept full responsibility for their projects. Only when this is achieved is it useful to help them to acquire capabilities based on the four principles of successful project sponsorship.

Changing convictions and behaviour requires a safe learning environment that, when needed, allows a person to look to themself for the cause. Therefore, in contradiction to what is sometimes presumed, combined training sessions for project sponsors and project managers should be avoided. Work with business managers only in small groups that allow a highly interactive approach.

In order to prevent the 'in our organization it doesn't work like that' reaction, work with real-life cases brought in by the participants.

Tip for the PRINCE2 environment

In the PRINCE2 environment the project sponsor is called project executive, so you might call the training 'PRINCE2 for the project executive'.

Most PRINCE2 principles are formulated as an imperative, such as 'manage by exception' or 'focus on products'. However, two of them are formulated in a descriptive way: 'continued business justification' and 'defined roles and responsibilities'. For project sponsors these happen to be the two most important ones, equivalent to the first two principles of successful project sponsorship as defined in this book. The disadvantage of the descriptive wording of these principles is that it does not appeal to the personal responsibility of the project sponsor. In a training situation, people sometimes react to them with 'we don't have that' or 'in our company it doesn't work this way'. Consider rephrasing them using an imperative. For example, 'take care of continued business justification' and 'define roles and responsibilities'.

This book can very well be used when implementing PRINCE2 in an organization. Each of the four principles of successful project sponsorship has one or more corresponding PRINCE2 principles, as illustrated in Table 14.1.

TABLE 14.1 Principles of successful project sponsorship and corresponding PRINCE2 principles

The Four Principles of Successful Project Sponsorship	Corresponding PRINCE2 Principles
1 Share the business case	Continued business justification
2 Organize ownership	Defined roles and responsibilities
3 Focus on deliverables	Focus on products
4 Empower the project manager	Manage by stages Manage by exception

Training the project managers

The main aim of including project managers in an initiative focused on advancing project sponsorship is to help them see their projects

Looking through the eyes of the sponsor

In Chapter 13 it was proposed that you ask the participants of a project sponsorship training course (before or at the start of the training course) what obstructions they encounter when trying to make a success of their project. It is advisable to train the project managers after you have trained the project sponsors, because this allows you to use the answers of the project sponsors to this question as input for the training for project managers. Before presenting them, ask the project managers what answers they expect the project sponsors from their organization to have given to this question (you can divide the group into subgroups and make it a contest – which group guesses most). Confronting the project managers' expectations with the real project sponsors' answers is a very instructive experience for the participants in order to understand what projects look like through the eyes of a project sponsor.

through the eyes of a project sponsor and, when relevant, to help them break the circle of dependence of project managers assuming project ownership and project sponsors avoiding it.

One of the main challenges for project managers often is to critically reflect on their own project ownership behaviour and how this effectively keeps their project sponsor from assuming full ownership. The aim is to stop this game of two people confirming each other in their complementary behaviour.

For project managers these insights into the project sponsor's role and how they relate to it are the starting point for improvement. It is important for project managers to practise how to support their project sponsor in the application of the four principles of successful project sponsorship, instead of taking over their responsibilities. Within the context of a training course for project managers this is best achieved by holding some brief workshops based on the participants' own cases, in order for them to experience how application of these principles indeed could improve the project sponsor's comfort by bringing more transparency into their project and making it easier to give strategic direction.

The fourth principle of successful project sponsorship, *empower the project manager*, is especially relevant for project managers. It helps them to understand exactly what decisions should be made by the steering group and what decisions should be made by themselves. This is an important foundation for successful cooperation with the project sponsor and the steering group.

Training the auditors

In operational management, repeatable processes play a key role. Quality management and auditing have a strong focus on ensuring that the operations comply with the quality system and deliver predictable outcomes. When auditors with a background in operational auditing switch to project auditing, one of the main pitfalls is the belief that a project will be successful if it carefully sticks to the application of a project management method. This easily leads to so-called 'checklist auditing' focused on the presence and completeness of documents. Projects, however, are not just a matter of repeatable processes with predictable outcomes. Indeed project management knows standardized processes, but the success of projects to a large extent depends on initiative, creativity, leadership and cooperation, and on knowing when not to adhere to the standardized processes.

The main purpose of project auditing is to check if a project is on the right course towards realizing its business case. From this perspective it is important for project auditors to see that, for instance, a steering group member who is really understanding and taking their responsibility might be more relevant than the issue register being fully up to date. This requires acceptance of the fact that project auditing itself cannot be fully standardized. Part of the auditors' attention should shift from the quality of documents to the human factor, and the use of checklists should partially be replaced by peer reviews between auditors.

Training the controllers

Controllers often have been educated as financial professionals with a strong focus on ensuring the financial integrity of an organization and on cost management. Project control, however, requires a broader perspective.

In a project environment the unpredictability of non-financial factors and their impact on the financial status of the project is relatively high. If, for instance, the financial figures of a project show that the project is on budget, but at the same time the issue register contains a number of open issues with an unknown financial impact, the financial figures are questionable. This implies that, in order to make a statement about the financial integrity of the project administration, a controller should be able to assess the quality of the issue register and the risk register and relate non-financial facts to the financial status.

In addition to this, projects are based on a business case. This business case in general will contain financial costs as well as financial and non-financial benefits, while the financial benefits often depend on the non-financial ones. A one-sided focus on cost management is therefore counterproductive. In a project environment costs are less predictable than in an operational environment and should permanently be weighed against financial and non-financial benefits. In order to assess the credibility of proposed financial benefits it is necessary to assess their dependency on non-financial benefits.

In summary, when controllers shift to project control, they will often need a broadening of perspective from financial to non-financial factors and their interdependencies, and from costs to benefits.

Steering group start-up meetings

A powerful aid in advancing project direction is to hold steering group start-up meetings. A steering group start-up meeting is a workshop held at the beginning of a project with the members of the steering group plus the project manager. This is where the four principles of successful project sponsorship all come together:

- the creation of a shared insight into the essence of the business case (a business case one-liner) and the priorities in project direction derived from it;
- the establishment of clearly understood roles of each steering group member, including each one's responsibility regarding stakeholder communication, benefit realization, risk ownership, quality control, resource availability and cost management;
- a common understanding of the project deliverables, their quality requirements and who is going to check them;
- a productive relationship between the steering group and the project manager, based on a clear empowerment of the latter.

In order to allow all participants to fully take part in the process, it is advisable to have steering group start-up meetings to be led by an independent facilitator. When needed, similar meetings can be held at stage transitions and to lay a new foundation for a project that has gone off the rails.

How to make a business case one-liner[1]

As described in Chapter 1, a business case one-liner (the summary of the business case in one sentence) is the basis for effective project communication. Of course this one-liner does not replace the full business case document: wherever needed, you use this document to underpin the one-liner.

So how do you make a powerful and distinctive one-liner for your project? It is essential that it is supported by those who have business responsibility for the project. Therefore it is useless if someone writes this one-liner on their own at their desk. The steering group, representing the most relevant stakeholders, if engaged in creation of the one-liner will experience it as a powerful communication tool and use it in its contact with other stakeholders. For a steering group, if facilitated well, the joint experience of formulating a catching one-liner can be a stimulating and engaging experience.

In order to gather the elements of a one-liner, ask each member of the steering group to answer the following three questions:

1 What is the main deliverable of the project?

2 What is the main reason why the organization invests in this project?

3 Imagine that it is five years after completion of this project and that you look back at the project from a distance: what effect do you see as the most relevant yardstick for its success?

The answers to these questions sometimes partially overlap. Still, due to the different angles, they usually lead to different results. It is important to come to a joint and accepted answer to each of these questions.[2] See to it that all participants can equally speak out about and are free to react to each of the questions, thus creating a great opportunity for the project sponsor to gain insight into the stakeholders' perceptions of the business case, enabling them to discuss it and explain their viewpoint where necessary. I have done this exercise with numerous steering groups and I am always amazed by the variety of answers and the impact of the discussions, even when a formal business case document has been discussed and approved. For the project sponsor the challenge in this process is to find the right balance between creating support among stakeholders (especially the steering group members) and one's own business case ownership.

Determining the essence[3]

An international manufacturing company is implementing the standard software package XYZ for the support of its logistic processes. The steering group is in a meeting to lay a good foundation for a project. Part of this meeting aims to clarify the business case with a one-liner, to be able to communicate it more effectively. This is relevant because in the perception of many employees the implementation of standard software is a purpose on its own. This perception undermines the support of the project.

What is the main deliverable?

To the question of what is the main deliverable of the project, the steering group members give the following answers:

- an effective and sustainable logistic process;
- implemented XYZ software;
- a world-class integrated logistic process;
- a logistic process that is respected (that is, effectively used) by everyone.

After some structured discussion the steering group decides that an integrated logistic process is the best representation of what should function after completion of the project.

What is the main reason?

To the question of what is the main reason behind the project, the steering group members give quite a variety of answers:

- to enable business improvement;
- to make an end to fragmentation of the organization;
- to extort uniform working processes;

- to improve on-time delivery;

- to improve key business processes;

- to improve operational efficiency;

- to implement the same processes consistently worldwide;

- to become the favourite supplier of our customers;

- to minimize business disruption.

It appears difficult to determine what is the main reason. On-time delivery and operational efficiency are the main candidates; both seem to play a central role. Therefore two hypothetical situations are discussed:

- Situation 1: suppose that, as a solution to a certain issue, a change is proposed that leads to a higher operational efficiency, but at the same time has a negative effect on the on-time delivery – would that basically be acceptable? All participants quickly come to an agreement on this; this would be unacceptable, because in the current situation customers are already leaving the company because of the unreliability of delivery times.

- Situation 2: the opposite – suppose that, as a solution to a certain issue, a change is proposed that leads to better on-time delivery, but at the same time has a negative effect on operational efficiency. Would that basically be acceptable? On this point the steering group members also quickly agree: yes, although reluctantly, such a choice could be imagined.

The conclusion of the steering group is that higher on-time delivery is the essence of the project and that project direction and communication should be focused on this. Of course this does not imply that operational efficiency is not a relevant additional goal.

What is the yardstick for success?

Finally, the yardstick for success. The project proposes several benefits, from higher operational efficiency to higher customer satisfaction. The steering group members, however, quickly agree on another yardstick for success. For the organization the project is a strategic investment and it is only successful if it contributes to the improvement of company performance.

One-liner

Based on the answers to the three questions – an integrated logistic process, higher on-time delivery and the improvement of company performance – the following one-liner is defined: 'An integrated logistic process to improve business performance through higher on-time delivery.'

With this one-liner everyone understands what is the essence of the project and how the project is related to corporate interests. The decisive criterion in decision-making about solutions or changes is now clear. This also will help users to understand why in some cases it is expected that they adapt their way of working to the selected software package, even if this new software supports their direct needs less than the old tailor-made software they were used to working with.

Summary

As part of a change initiative aiming to advance project sponsorship in an organization, several types of training course and workshop can be held, each with their own target group and goals:

- training for the board of directors to come to an insight into how the behaviour of the board of directors influences the achievements of the business managers of their organization in their roles as project sponsors;

- training for the project sponsors and steering group members to accept full responsibility for their projects and help them acquire capabilities based on the four principles of successful project sponsorship presented in this book;

- training for the project managers to help them see their projects through the eyes of a project sponsor and, when relevant, to stop confirming project sponsors in their behaviour of not assuming full ownership of their projects;

- training for the auditors to see that project success to a large extent does not depend on sticking to a project management method but on initiative, creativity, leadership and co-operation, and to learn how to focus project auditing on the chances of a project to achieve its business case;

- training for the controllers to broaden their perspective from costs to benefits and to include non-financial factors and their relationship to financial factors in their approach;

- steering group start-up meetings to come to a shared insight into the business case, clear roles and responsibilities for steering group members, a common understanding of the project deliverables and a productive relationship with the project manager.

Notes

1 Translated from 'Waarom doen we dit eigenlijk? De businesscase als succesfactor van projecten' (Why are we doing this? The business case as project success factor) (Van der Molen, 2013).

2 A useful aid to achieve this is the nominal group technique, a process that can be used in groups to come to a quick decision, but taking into account everyone's opinion, as opposed to traditional voting, where only the largest group is considered. After every member of the group has given their answer to a question (with a short explanation), duplicate answers are eliminated and the members rank the answers. As a result of integration of the ranking results, the most supported solution comes on top. Advantages of the nominal group technique are that it involves participation of all the members of the group, that it is very efficient and avoids the need for discussions, and that it mostly leads to a well-supported result. See http://en.wikipedia.org/wiki/Nominal_group_technique.

3 Translated from 'Waarom doen we dit eigenlijk? De businesscase als succesfactor van projecten' (Why are we doing this? The business case as project success factor) (Van der Molen, 2013).

Summary of
Part 3

The main challenge when advancing project sponsorship in organizations is truly to create business ownership of projects. Crucial is an integrated approach focused on the behaviour of all groups involved: the board of directors; the project sponsors and other business managers taking part in steering groups; the project managers; the project auditors; and the project controllers. Advancing project sponsorship will often require that the organization's performance management, management development, quality system and project budgets are adapted. Rather than this being a temporary endeavour it requires continuous effort.

Epilogue

Even if you put all the principles and tips in this book into practice, in a complex, rapidly changing and never fully known environment project execution will always be different from what you expected. Keep in mind that a successful project is not necessarily fully completed according to schedule and budget. What counts is that, amidst changes, you work with the project's stakeholders to maintain a focus on optimum support of corporate objectives as defined in the project's business case. In doing so, I hope this book may support and inspire you.

APPENDIX 1
PMBOK overview[1]

What is the PMBOK?

The PMBOK (Project Management Body of Knowledge) is a set of standard terminology and guidelines for project management laid down in the *PMBOK Guide*, published by the Project Management Institute (PMI), the world's leading association for project managers. PMBOK is a trademark of Project Management Institute, Inc.

The PMBOK is not a project management method, but a foundational reference for the application of project management knowledge and good practices. It can serve as a framework for the development of a project management method or for the definition of an approach to a specific project.

History and adoption

The first edition of the *PMBOK Guide* was published by the Project Management Institute in 1996. The fifth edition appeared in 2013.

In 2008 the *PMBOK Guide* was recognized as a standard by the American National Standards Institute (ANSI). In 2011 it was recognized as a standard by the Institute of Electrical and Electronics Engineers (IEEE).

The *PMBOK Guide* has obtained a global spread, with a dominant position in the United States, the Far East and parts of Europe. In 2012 the International Organization for Standardization (ISO) adopted the main structure and the majority of the process-related content of the *PMBOK Guide* when issuing the latest global standard on project management, ISO 21500:2012, guidance on project management.

Content

The *PMBOK Guide* (fifth edition) defines 47 processes that fall into five basic process groups and 10 knowledge areas.

The five process groups are:

- *Initiating*: those processes performed to define a new project or a new phase of an existing project by obtaining authorization to start the project or phase.

- *Planning*: those processes required to establish the scope of the project, refine the objectives, and define the course of action required to attain the objectives that the project was undertaken to achieve.

- *Executing*: those processes performed to complete the work defined in the project management plan to satisfy the project specifications.

- *Monitoring and controlling*: those processes required to track, review and regulate the progress and performance of the project, identify any areas in which changes to the plan are required and initiate the corresponding changes.

- *Closing*: those processes performed to finalize all activities across all process groups to formally close the project or phase.[2]

The 10 knowledge areas are:

- *Project integration management*: includes the processes and activities needed to identify, define, combine, unify, and coordinate the various processes and project management activities within the process groups.

- *Project scope management*: includes the processes required to ensure that the project includes all the work required, and only the work required, to complete the project successfully.

- *Project time management*: includes the processes required to manage the timely completion of the project.

- *Project cost management*: includes the processes involved in planning, estimating, budgeting, financing, funding, managing, and controlling costs so that the project can be completed within the approved budget.

- *Project quality management*: includes the processes and activities of the performing organization that determine quality policies, objectives and responsibilities so that the project will satisfy the needs for which it was undertaken.

- *Project human resource management*: includes the processes that organize, manage and lead the project team.

- *Project communications management*: includes the processes that are required to ensure timely and appropriate planning, collection, creation, distribution, storage, retrieval, management, control, monitoring and the ultimate disposition of project information.

- *Project risk management*: includes the processes of conducting risk management planning, identification, analysis, response planning and controlling risk on a project.

- *Project procurement management*: includes the processes necessary to purchase or acquire products, services or results needed from outside the project team.

- *Project stakeholder management*: includes the processes required to identify all people or organizations impacted by the project, analysing stakeholder expectations and impact on the project, and developing appropriate management strategies for effectively engaging stakeholders in project decisions and execution.[3]

Each of the 10 knowledge areas contains the project management processes that need to be accomplished within its discipline in order to achieve effective project management. Each of these processes also falls into one of the five process groups. In this way a matrix structure is created such that every process can be related to one knowledge area and one process group. The project management processes create outputs (the project management plan and other project documents), which makes the project management tangible.

Pros and cons

The strength of the *PMBOK Guide* is that it is the most widely used global project management standard, which makes it suitable as a common framework for international and/or cross-organizational cooperation in projects. Its generic nature makes it suitable for almost any type of project. The fact that the guide is under control of the leading international professional organization for project management professionals guarantees that it will stay in line with the common interests of the project management profession.

As a result of its roots (the project manager's practice), the *PMBOK Guide* is developed from a project manager's perspective and stands close to the natural way of thinking of project managers, which makes it easy to adopt. As a consequence, however, it has a limited definition of project success: it is measured by product and project quality, timeliness, budget compliance and degree of customer satisfaction. As discussed in the Introduction to this book, for a project sponsor a project is an investment and as such only successful if its business case is realized.[4]

The *PMBOK Guide* offers limited support for project sponsors. It also offers little support for those project manager's tasks that are related to supporting the project sponsor and the steering group and to defining the project manager's authority in relation to the steering group. A good project manager should be able to advise their project sponsor about topics such as business case development and maintenance, steering group composition, the organization and preparation of steering group decision-making and the creation of benefit ownership in order to enhance stakeholder engagement. A project manager should also be able to propose a definition of their own authority: what they can decide and account for retrospectively, and what they should escalate immediately. These subjects are not included in the knowledge areas of the PMBOK.

Notes

1 Sources: *A Guide to the Project Management Body of Knowledge (PMBOK® Guide)*, 5th edition (PMI, 2013a), *A Pocket Companion to PMI's PMBOK Guide* (Snijders, Wuttke and Zandhuis, 2013), Wikipedia.

2 The list is taken from *A Guide to the Project Management Body of Knowledge (PMBOK® Guide)*, 5th edition (PMI, 2013a).

3 Taken from *A Guide to the Project Management Body of Knowledge (PMBOK® Guide)*, 5th edition (PMI, 2013a).

4 Managing the realization of the business case is outside the scope of the PMBOK. In case it appears that the realization of the business case is too complex to be transferred back immediately to the sponsoring organization, in the concepts of PMI business case realization is then typically done via a programme (PMI, 2013b).

APPENDIX 2
PRINCE2 overview[1]

What is PRINCE2?

PRINCE2 (Projects in Controlled Environments 2) is a project management method and a trademark of Axelos Ltd. While most other project management methods see project management as a competence of project managers – and are an answer to the question 'what can a project manager do to turn a project into a success?' – PRINCE2 is based on the viewpoint that project management is a competence of an organization and answers the question 'what can several stakeholders, among which the project sponsor, steering group members, project manager and team managers, do to turn a project into a success?' It has a strong focus on the alignment of the project with corporate strategy.

PRINCE2 is not a ready-made method; it should be tailored to suit the needs of a specific organization and project.

History and adoption

In 1989, the British Central Computer and Telecommunications Agency (CCTA) developed PRINCE (Projects in Controlled Environments) as the standard method for effective project management for all British government information and communication technology (ICT) projects. The ownership of the method was taken over by the Office of Government Commerce (OGC), who transformed it into a generic project management method and renamed it PRINCE2, first released in 1996. The method had several updates, the last of which appeared in 2009. The OGC was succeeded by HM Cabinet Office who sold the rights in 2013 to Axelos Ltd, a joint venture of HM Cabinet Office and Capita plc.

PRINCE2 is rooted in large public sector organizations and has been adopted in other industries. It has a global spread, with a dominant position in several Western European countries.

Content

PRINCE2 defines seven principles that are seen as fundamental for good professional practice, seven themes that can be compared to the knowledge areas of the PMBOK, and a process model that can be compared with the processes of the PMBOK.

The seven principles are:

- A project has *continued business justification*.
- Project teams *learn from previous experience* (lessons are sought, recorded and acted upon throughout the life of the project).
- A project has *defined and agreed roles and responsibilities* with an organization structure that engages the business, user and supplier stakeholder interests.
- A project is planned, monitored and controlled on a stage-by-stage basis (*management by stages*).
- A project has defined tolerances for each project objective to establish limits of delegated authority (*management by exception*).
- A project focuses on the definition and delivery of *products*, in particular their scope and quality requirements.
- PRINCE2 is *tailored* to suit the project's environment, size, complexity, importance, capability and risk.[2]

The seven themes are those aspects of project management that need to be addressed continually, integrated in many processes. The themes are business case, organization, quality, plans, risk, change and progress.

The PRINCE2 process model addresses project activity at four levels of management:

- *corporate or programme management*, which sets the business context for projects;
- *the project board (steering group)*, accountable for the success of the project within the boundaries set by corporate or programme management;
- *the project manager*, responsible for the day-to-day management of the project within constraints approved by the project board;
- *the team manager*, supervising the creation of the products allocated to the team by the project manager (in simple projects this role and the role of project manager are performed by the same person).

The PRINCE2 process model contains the following processes:

- *Starting up a project*, covering the pre-project activities required to commission the project and to get commitment from corporate or programme management to invest in it.
- *Directing a project*, describing the project board's activities in making key decisions and exercising overall project control, while delegating the day-to-day management to the project manager.
- *Initiating a project*, describing the activities that the project manager must lead in order to establish the project on a sound foundation, including an overall project plan containing baselines for time, cost, quality, scope, risk and benefits.
- *Managing a stage boundary*, describing what the project manager must undertake to provide the project board with the information necessary to decide to continue to the next stage of the project.
- *Controlling a stage*, describing how the project manager manages project execution during a stage and report progress and exceptions to the project board.

- *Managing product delivery*, addressing the team manager's role in supervising the creation of the products.

- *Closing a project*, describing the closure activities towards the end of the project including any remaining project acceptance and handover requirements.[3]

Pros and cons

As a result of its roots (public sector organizations in their role as sponsoring organizations), PRINCE2 is based on a wider perspective than just that of the project manager: among others it also supports the roles of senior management, the project sponsor and the steering group members, with a strong focus on business alignment of the project based on its business case. This is the 'controlled environment' that the acronym refers to and it offers useful support for advancing project management in organizations.

A disadvantage of PRINCE2 is that it is a commercial product, a source of royalties for its owners and of surplus margins for accredited training companies who are licensed to sell PRINCE2 training courses and exams. Instead of being interested in integrating PRINCE2, PMBOK and other standards into one common framework and language, these parties have a business interest to distinguish themselves from the rest of the project management community.[4] This is not always in the interest of the global project management community.[5]

A risk of PRINCE2 is that, in the hands of inexperienced staff, a docile application of this extensive method may lead to an unnecessary bureaucracy that is counterproductive to the success of a project.

Notes

1 Sources: *Directing Successful Projects with PRINCE2*™ (OGC, 2009), Wikipedia.

2 Taken from *Directing Successful Projects with PRINCE2*™ (OGC, 2009).

3 Taken from *Directing Successful Projects with PRINCE2™* (OGC, 2009).

4 In 2012 the International Standardization Organization (ISO) released the ISO 21500 Guidance on Project Management. The owners of PRINCE2 so far have made no known attempts to influence this guidance in their direction or to adapt PRINCE2 to this guidance.

5 As an example, see the Wikipedia item on PRINCE2, which has been a battleground of conflicting interests for many years already.

APPENDIX 3
Agile overview[1]

What is agile?

Agile is not a method or approach but a collective name for a number of approaches among which are scrum, extreme programming, extreme manufacturing and crystal clear.

Agile refers to an iterative and incremental approach to managing the design and build activities for engineering, information technology and new product or service development projects in a highly flexible and interactive manner, for example agile software development. It requires capable individuals from the customer as well as the supplier side.

Agile is seen as the opposite of the classic waterfall approach in which progress is seen as flowing steadily downwards (like a waterfall) through the phases of conception, initiation, analysis, design, construction, testing, production/implementation and maintenance. The main argument against the waterfall approach is that it is too inflexible. In a complex and dynamic environment it is impossible to make a perfect analysis and design, and when at a later stage a change of requirements appears to be necessary a lot of work has to be redone at high cost. As an alternative the agile approach divides a project into very small iterations, each of which contain the analysis, design, construction, testing and implementation of a small piece of functionality.

History and adoption

Long before the introduction of the term agile in this context, the basics of what is now labelled as agile were seen as common sense by many software development professionals and implemented in early agile methods such as scrum and DSDM. In 2001, as a reaction to the failure of formal software development methods based on the waterfall approach, a group of software developers published the agile manifesto:

> We are uncovering better ways of developing software by doing it and helping others do it. Through this work we have come to value:
>
> - individuals and interactions over processes and tools;
> - working software over comprehensive documentation;
> - customer collaboration over contract negotiation;
> - responding to change over following a plan.
>
> That is, while there is value in the items on the right, we value the items on the left more.[2]

The agile manifesto is based on 12 principles:

- Our highest priority is to satisfy the customer through early and continuous delivery of valuable software.

- Welcome changing requirements, even late in development. Agile processes harness change for the customer's competitive advantage.

- Deliver working software frequently, from a couple of weeks to a couple of months, with a preference to the shorter timescale.

- Business people and developers must work together daily throughout the project.

- Build projects around motivated individuals. Give them the environment and support they need, and trust them to get the job done.

- The most efficient and effective method of conveying information to and within a development team is face-to-face conversation.

- Working software is the primary measure of progress.

- Agile processes promote sustainable development. The sponsors, developers and users should be able to maintain a constant pace indefinitely.

- Continuous attention to technical excellence and good design enhances agility.
- Simplicity – the art of maximizing the amount of work not done – is essential.
- The best architectures, requirements and designs emerge from self-organizing teams.
- At regular intervals, the team reflects on how to become more effective, then tunes and adjusts its behaviour accordingly.[3]

In the ICT industry, the agile approach is very popular worldwide among ICT professionals while gaining increasing acceptance at management level, on the supplier side as well as on the customer side. In other industries the agile approach has gained significant popularity as a way to speed up and improve quality, especially in the design stages of projects.

Content

As mentioned, the agile approach is reflected in a number of approaches, each with their own practices and terminology. Some of the most well-known agile concepts are:

- *Iterative development*: the development of a solution through repeated cycles of analyse–design–realize–check (iterations, also called sprints), each iteration leading to a better solution than the previous one.
- *Continuous planning and reprioritization*: this enables learning from experience and optimizing the business value in a dynamic environment.
- *Development team*: a team of users and specialists working closely together on a solution, instead of specialists making a solution and users having to accept it.
- *Work item*: defined amount of work to be realized by the development team (in each iteration several work items can be realized).
- *Product backlog (project backlog)*: prioritized list of work items.

- *Product owner*: the individual representing the users, empowered to set priorities in the product backlog and to formally accept realized work items.
- *Stand-up meeting*: short meeting, held literally standing up in order to keep people from talking too long, with emphasis on face-to-face contact and direct decision-making.
- *Time-boxing*: doing what can be done within a certain amount of time instead of focusing on a predefined deliverable.

Pros and cons

Advantages of a well-implemented agile approach are:

- Optimized business value through permanent reprioritization.
- Better quality and smooth handover to operations through intensive user participation and permanent testing.
- Lower cost of development because of more flexible responses to growing insight (the need for rework, a typical effect of growing insight in a waterfall approach, is reduced).

An agile approach is not suitable for all stages of all projects. For reasons of safety or legislation – such as in medical or space technology – documented control may be more important than flexibility, cost-efficiency and permanent improvement. And in the realization stage of some projects – such as the building of a bridge – for quite some time the exact execution of the plan is more relevant than permanent learning and adapting.

In order to be successful an agile approach requires experienced specialists with highly developed technical and communication skills, and engaged user representatives.

Notes

1 Sources: *This is Agile* (Hoogendoorn, 2014); Wikipedia, http://agilemanifesto.org/.

2 Quoted from http://agilemanifesto.org.

3 Quoted from http://agilemanifesto.org.

APPENDIX 4
Responsibilities and accountabilities

This appendix gives an overview of the main responsibilities and accountabilities related to the direction and management of a project (Figure A4.1). This overview can be seen as a default, to be deviated from depending on the project and its context.

In case there is no steering group:

- The responsibilities and accountabilities assigned to the senior user should be assigned to the project sponsor.

- The responsibilities and accountabilities assigned to the senior supplier should be assigned to the external contractor or the management of the internal supplying department, with whom the project sponsor can communicate on a bilateral basis.

In case portfolio management and/or programme management are in place in your organization, important steering group responsibilities mentioned in this appendix may be fulfilled by a portfolio manager or programme manager. Typically, the availability of specialist staff is a concern to be addressed at portfolio level, whereas user engagement and the implementation of benefit management are concerns to address at programme level.

FIGURE A4.1 Overview of the main responsibilities and accountabilities related to the direction and management of a project

	Project Manager	Senior Supplier	Senior User	Project Sponsor	
Sharing the business case	R	R	R	R	A
Communication with corporate management				R	A
Guiding business case development					
Realization of the business case, achievement of the business goal of the project					
Steering group composition					
Chairing the steering group					
Assurance of business-related issues of project management					
Approval of plans and reports provided by the project manager					
Approval of changes, unless delegated to senior user, change control board or project manager					
Authorization of the start of the project and project phases					
Functioning of the change control board (or delegated to senior user)					
Authorization of project closure					
In the case of a commercial relationship					

	Project Manager	Senior Supplier	Senior User	Project Sponsor	
In the case of an internal project manager: • assignment of the project manager • continuity of the project management role • decommissioning of the project manager In the case of a supplier-provided project manager (this can be delegated to an internal senior supplier): • the approval of the supplier contract • decommissioning of the supplier				R	A
Availability of users for participation in the project (definition of requirements, specification, co-creation, testing, acceptance) Ensure unambiguity of the user's viewpoint Ensure user engagement (grass-root support) Assurance of user-related issues of project management Advise the project manager on user-related issues, including stakeholder engagement Implementation of benefit management			R	A	

(Continued)

FIGURE A4.1 *(Continued)*

	Project Manager	Senior Supplier	Senior User	Project Sponsor
Availability of specialist staff		R		A
Supplier engagement (main contractor function at contract level)				
Advise the project manager on supplier-related issues				
Assurance of supplier-related issues of project management				
In the case of a supplier-provided project manager:				
• assignment of the project manager				
• continuity of the project management role				
• decommissioning of the project manager				
Daily management of the project, directing subcontractors, taking corrective action within tolerances	R			A
Achievement of the project objective				
Liaison with related projects				
Organizing risk management				
Development of plans (project management plan and all its components such as schedule management plan, cost management plan, quality management plan; eventually stage plans)				

	Project Manager	Senior Supplier	Senior User	Project Sponsor
Maintenance of registers (issue register, risk register, quality control measurements) Timely and reliable reporting (performance reports, exception reports, end stage reports, end project reports)	R			A
Correct specification of user needs Alignment of solution with business processes, delivery of functional quality, user acceptance of the project deliverables Stakeholder communication (to users)	R		A*	
Compliance of the project to budget, schedule, specifications and quality standards, delivery of technical quality Main contractor at operational level Stakeholder communication (to suppliers)	R	A*		
Keeping an eye on a specific risk and undertaking action when a risk occurs (each person can be responsible for one or more specific risks)	R	R	R	R A

*The final accountability for the project as a whole, including the assignment of senior user and senior supplier roles, lies with the project sponsor.

APPENDIX 5
A note on the terminology used in this book

Basic choice

This book aims to support business managers in their role as project sponsor, regardless of the project management framework, method or techniques used by the project manager and regardless of whether the project is executed by an internal or an external supplier.

It is necessary though to make choices in terminology and definitions. In order to align this book to the most commonly used terminology, I chose to use the terms and definitions of the Project Management Body of Knowledge (PMBOK), the globally most widely accepted project management framework (see Appendix 1, page 209).

Alternative terms for other environments

The second most used project management glossary is that of PRINCE2 (see Appendix 2, page 214). In order to help readers from this environment I have added alternative terms in parentheses, and tips where relevant.

The Glossary to this book contains the (mainly PMBOK) terms used in this book plus, where applicable, the corresponding PRINCE2 term and other popular alternatives.

Agile is not a method with a glossary, but an approach to projects so different that it affects the basic concepts presented in this book (see Appendix 3, page 219). For readers involved in agile projects there are tips explaining the differences.

Exceptions

There are a few exceptions to my basic choice regarding terminology. One exception is the use of the terms *customer* and *supplier*. The PMBOK glossary defines the customer as 'the person(s) or organization(s) that will pay for the project's product, service or result. Customers can be internal or external to the performing organization'. The performing organization is defined as 'an enterprise whose personnel are most directly involved in doing the work of the project or programme'. The term supplier is not defined. By not defining a supplier, and defining the customer in their relationship to the 'performing organization', in my opinion these definitions implicitly represent a supplier perspective on projects (although this may be hard to see for someone who is used to thinking from such a perspective). This can best be explained by describing the reverse, a customer perspective. This would be not to define a customer but to define a sponsoring organization as 'the organization funding the project and whose personnel are most directly involved in defining the requirements, accepting the deliverables and putting them into operation in order to realize the benefits', and to define a supplier in their relationship to this sponsoring organization as 'the person(s) or organization(s) that make a living from working on the project. Suppliers can be internal or external to the sponsoring organization.'

Because I strive to use language that suits all stakeholders I have tried to choose terminology from a neutral perspective, defining roles not in their relationship to a specific party (neither the performing organization nor the sponsoring organization) but in their relationship to the project deliverable:

- the project sponsor, investing in it;
- the user, using it;
- and the supplier, supplying it.

All three roles can be performed by people from the same or different organizations.

Another exception is the definition of project success. The PMBOK measures project success by product and project quality, timeliness, budget compliance and degree of customer satisfaction. I see this as a project manager's perspective. From the project sponsor's perspective a project is an investment and hence only successful if its business goal is realized as defined in the business case. Actually, what it takes to achieve this makes for an important part of this book. This is reflected in the definition of project success given in the Introduction.

Additional terms

In order to describe the interfaces between the project and its environment I had to add terminology that is not part of the glossary of the PMBOK. Examples are: project assurance, senior user, senior supplier, risk owner, benefit owner, stakeholder relationship owner, management stage, tolerance, exception and exception report.

For full definitions of the terms referred to in this explanation see the Glossary (page 231).

GLOSSARY

This glossary contains preferred as well as alternative terms. I have given preference to terms and definitions as listed in PMI's Lexicon of Project Management Terms. I have abbreviated, clarified or otherwise adapted some of their definitions to the needs of this book and its target group. Alternative terms (such as PRINCE2 terms) are presented in parentheses. These are not necessarily exact synonyms but in my opinion they are corresponding concepts. For details on the use of terminology see Appendix 5 (page 228).

Acceptance criteria: A set of conditions that is required to be met before deliverables are accepted.

Accountability: The obligation of an individual or organization to account for its activities or achievements. Accountability cannot be shared. Typically one can be held accountable for the outcomes of activities of oneself and one's subordinates. To be compared with responsibility.

Activity: A distinct, scheduled portion of work performed during the course of a project.

Agile project approach: An iterative and incremental approach to managing the design and build activities for engineering, information technology, and new product or service development projects in a highly flexible and interactive manner.

Approver: A person or group authorized to formally release a deliverable.

Assurance: A mechanism that ensures that when issues occur corrective action will be taken. A relevant feature of an assurance mechanism is that it is relatively independent of the process it assures.

Baseline: The approved version of a work product (such as a schedule, requirement or deliverable) that can be changed only through a formal change control procedure and is used as a basis for comparison.

Benefit: An effect (outcome) of a project seen as positive by a stakeholder.

Benefit owner: A person who is responsible and feels responsible to realize a specific benefit.

Budget: Cost estimate. In popular language and in this book often used as a synonym of cost baseline.

Business assurance: Assurance from a business perspective, by or on behalf of the project sponsor.

Business case: The justification or motivation of the project. Also see business case document.

Business case document: A document describing the business case of a project, typically containing costs, benefits, risks and timescales. Also see business case.

Business deliverable: See deliverable.

Business executive: See project sponsor.

Business product: See deliverable.

Business result: The outcome of a project seen from a business perspective, including the realization of the benefits. The accountability of the project sponsor. To be compared with project result.

Change authority: A person appointed by the steering group authorized within boundaries to approve or reject change requests.

Change budget: A budget for the execution of approved change requests.

Change control: A process whereby modifications to documents or deliverables that are part of the baseline are identified, documented, approved or rejected.

Change control board: A group appointed by the steering group authorized within boundaries to approve or reject change requests.

Change request (request for change): A formal proposal to modify a document or deliverable that is part of the baseline.

Communication management strategy: See communications management plan.

Communication plan: See communications management plan.

Communications management plan (communication plan, communication management strategy): A component of the project management plan that describes how, when and by whom communication with stakeholders will take place. Meaningful communication requires two-way traffic and cannot be planned in detail.

Constraint: A limiting factor that affects the execution of a project, programme, portfolio or process.

Corrective action: In case of an issue: an intentional activity that realigns the performance of the project work with the project management plan or reduces the impact.

Cost baseline: The approved version of the time-phased project budget, excluding any management reserves, which can be changed only through formal change control procedures and is used as a basis for comparison to actual results.

Customer's quality expectations: See high-level requirements.

Deliverable (business product): Any unique and verifiable product, result or capability to perform a service that is required to be produced to complete a process, phase or project.

Development team: In an agile project approach: a team of users and specialists working closely together on a solution, instead of specialists making a solution and users having to accept it.

Deviation: The difference between realization and baseline.

Earned value: The measure of work performed expressed in terms of the budget authorized for that work.

Earned value management: A methodology that combines scope, schedule and resource measurements to assess project performance and progress.

End product: See project result.

End project report: A report given by the project manager to the steering group that confirms the handover of all deliverables and provides an assessment of how well the project has performed against the original project plan.

End stage report: A report given by the project manager to the steering group at the end of each management stage of the project, providing an assessment of how well the project has performed during a stage and the project status at stage end.

Exception: A situation where it can be forecast that there will be a deviation beyond the tolerance levels agreed between the project manager and the steering group.

Exception plan: A plan to replace an existing plan.

Exception report: A report given by the project manager to the steering group in the case of a deviation beyond tolerance, containing a description of the exception situation, its impact, options, recommendation and impact of the recommendation.

External product: A deliverable outside the scope of the project, but necessary to realize one or more deliverables that are in the scope of the project. External products can be delivered by another project organization or a line organization.

High-level requirements (customer's quality expectations): The requirements of the end deliverable of the project defined as part of the project charter. Framework for the quality to be realized by the project, relevant to make sure that this quality will meet the expectations of sponsors and users.

Highlight report: See performance report.

Initiation stage: See planning phase.

Issue: A relevant event that has happened, was not planned and requires management action.

Issue log: See issue register.

Issue register (issue log): A registration of all issues, for each issue containing a description of the impact, decision made and current status.

Iterative development: The development of a solution through repeated cycles of analyse–design–realize–check (iterations, also called sprints), each iteration leading to a better solution than the previous one.

Lessons learned: The knowledge gained during a project, which shows how project events were addressed or should be addressed in the future for the purpose of improving future performance.

Management by exception: In the context of project direction by the steering group: approach based on defined tolerances for the project manager (limits of delegated authority) enabling each decision to be made at the appropriate management level, thus allowing the most efficient use of senior management time without removing their control.

Management product: Document delivered by the project only needed to direct or manage the project, such as a project plan or a performance report. To be compared with business deliverable.

Management reserve: An amount of the project budget withheld by the steering group for management control purposes and reserved for the approval of change requests and/or unforeseen work that is within the scope of the project.

Management stage: A part of a project for which the steering group makes available a budget and defines authorities for the project manager.

Milestone: A significant point or event in a project, mostly the completion of a relevant deliverable.

Opportunity: A risk that would have a positive effect on one or more project objectives.

Ownership: The state of feeling and taking full responsibility to achieve a result. To be compared with responsibility.

PBS: See product breakdown structure.

Percentage complete: An estimate expressed as a percentage of the amount of work that has been completed on an activity, process or phase.

Performance report (highlight report, status report, progress report): A periodical report from the project manager to the project sponsor and the steering group, looking back on the past reporting period and looking forward to the coming period and comparing expectations regarding the end of the current stage with the baseline (the plan).

Performing organization: An enterprise whose personnel are the most directly involved in doing the work of the project or programme. Can be the same as the sponsoring organization.

PFD: See product flow diagram.

Plan: A detailed proposal for doing or achieving something.

Planning phase (initiation stage): First phase of the project, focused on elaborating among others the business case, the risk assessment, the schedule and budget.

PMBOK: See Project Management Body of Knowledge (PMBOK).

Portfolio: Projects, programmes, subportfolios and operations managed as a group to achieve strategic objectives.

Portfolio management: The centralized management of one or more portfolios to achieve strategic objectives.

PRINCE2 (PRojects IN Controlled Environments 2): A project management method and a trademark of Axelos Ltd.

Product: See deliverable.

Product backlog (project backlog): In an agile project approach: prioritized list of work items.

Product breakdown structure (PBS): A hierarchy of all the products to be produced during a plan.

Product flow diagram (PFD): A diagram showing the sequence of production and interdependencies of the products listed in a product breakdown structure.

Product-based planning: A technique leading to a comprehensive plan based on the creation and delivery of required outputs. The technique considers prerequisite products, quality requirements and the dependencies between products.

Product owner: In an agile project approach: the individual representing the users, empowered to set priorities in the product backlog and to formally release solutions.

Programme: A group of related projects, subprogrammes and line management activities that are managed in a coordinated way to obtain benefits not available from managing them individually.

Programme management: The application of knowledge, skills, tools and techniques to a programme to meet the programme requirements and to obtain benefits and control not available by managing projects individually.

Progress report: See performance report.

Project: A temporary endeavour undertaken to create a unique product, service or result, started by the sponsoring organization in order to achieve a business goal (a positive effect for itself or its stakeholders).

Project assurance: Responsibility of the steering group to ensure that the project is managed and executed correctly.

Project backlog: See product backlog.

Project board: See steering group.

Project brief: See project charter.

Project charter (project brief): A document issued by the project initiator or sponsor that formally authorizes the existence of a project and sketches its outline.

Project executive: See project sponsor.

Project initiation documentation (PID): See project management plan.

Project management: The application of knowledge, skills, tools and techniques to project activities to meet the project requirements.

Project Management Body of Knowledge (PMBOK): A set of standard terminology and guidelines for project management laid down in the *PMBOK Guide*, published by the Project Management Institute (PMI), the world's leading association for project managers and a trademark of Project Management Institute, Inc.

Project management plan (project initiation documentation): The document that describes how the project will be executed, monitored and controlled, covering scope management, requirements management, schedule management, cost management and stakeholder management.

Project management success: Completion of the project within the constraints of scope, time, cost, quality, resources and risk as approved by the steering group. To be compared to project success.

Project management team: The members of the project team who are directly involved in project management activities. Beware of confusion: in PRINCE2 the same term refers to the entire management structure of the project, consisting of the project board (steering group), the project manager and any team manager, project assurance or project support roles.

Project manager: The person given the authority and responsibility to manage the project on a day-to-day basis to realize the required deliverables within the constraints agreed with the steering group.

Project owner: See project sponsor.

Project phase: A collection of logically related project activities that culminates in the completion of one or more deliverables.

Project result: The result achieved by the project manager, its deliverables. To be compared with business result.

Project scope: The work performed to deliver a product, service or result with the specified features and functions.

Project sponsor (project executive, business executive, executive, sponsor, project owner): The single individual who is responsible on behalf of the (permanent) line organization to direct the (temporary) project organization, representing the business interests in the direction of the project and accountable for the realization of its business case.

Project success: Realization of the business case of the project, the primary responsibility of the project sponsor. To be compared to project management success.

Project support: An administrative role in the project management team in the form of advice and help with project management tools, guidance, administrative services such as filing, the collection of actual data and/or the preparation of reports.

Quality: The degree to which a set of inherent characteristics fulfils requirements.

Quality activities: The process of monitoring specific deliverables to determine whether they comply with relevant standards and/or requirements.

Quality control: See quality activities.

Quality control measurements (quality register, quality log): The documented results of quality activities.

Quality log: See quality control measurements.

Quality management plan (quality management strategy, quality plan): A component of the project management plan that describes how an organization's quality policies will be implemented.

Quality management strategy: See quality management plan.

Quality plan: See quality management plan.

Quality register: See quality control measurements.

Request for change: See change request.

Requirement: A condition or capability that is required to be present in a product, service or result to satisfy a formally imposed specification.

Responsibility: A duty or obligation to satisfactorily perform or complete a task (assigned by someone, or created by one's own promise or circumstances) that one must fulfil. Responsibilities can be shared. One can take responsibility. To be compared with accountability.

Reviewer: An individual performing quality activities.

Risk: An uncertain event or condition that, if it occurs, has a positive or negative effect on one or more project objectives.

Risk category: A group of potential causes of risk.

Risk log: See risk register.

Risk management plan (risk management strategy): A component of the project management plan that describes how risk management activities will be structured and performed.

Risk management strategy: See risk management plan.

Risk mitigation: A risk response strategy whereby the project team acts to reduce the probability of occurrence or impact of a risk.

Risk owner: An individual who is responsible for the management, monitoring and control of all aspects of a particular risk assigned to them, including the implementation of the selected responses to address the threats or to maximize the opportunities.

Risk register (risk log): A document in which the results of risk analysis and risk response planning are recorded.

Schedule: Graphical representation of a plan that presents linked activities with planned dates, durations, milestones and resources. In popular language, and in this book, often used as a synonym of schedule baseline.

Schedule baseline: The approved version of a schedule model that can be changed only through formal change control procedures and is used as a basis for comparison to actual results.

Scope: The sum of the products, services and results to be provided as a project. In popular language, as in this book, often used as a synonym of scope baseline.

Scope baseline: The approved version of a scope description, which can be changed only through formal change control procedures and is used as a basis for comparison.

Scope creep: The uncontrolled expansion of product or project scope without adjustments to time, cost and resources.

Senior supplier: The steering group role representing the supplier interests within the project and providing supplier resources, accountable for ensuring compliance of the project result with the baseline (scope, quality, schedule and budget). See the definition of supplier.

Senior user: The steering group role representing the user interests within the project and accountable for ensuring that user needs are specified correctly, that the solution meets those needs and that it enables the realization of the proposed benefits. See the definition of user.

Specification: A document that specifies the requirements, design, behaviour or other characteristics of a deliverable.

Sponsor: See project sponsor.

Sponsoring organization: The organization funding the project and whose personnel are most directly involved in defining the requirements, accepting the deliverables and putting them into operation in order to realize the benefits. Can be the same as the performing organization.

Stage plan: Detailed plan for managing a stage, including a schedule and a budget.

Stakeholder: An individual, group or organization that may affect, be affected by or perceive itself to be affected by a decision, activity or outcome of the project.

Stakeholder relationship owner: The steering group member who is responsible for the engagement of a specific stakeholder.

Stand-up meeting: Short meeting, held standing up in order to keep people from talking too long, with emphasis on face-to-face contact and direct decision-making.

Status report: See performance report.

Steering committee: See steering group.

Steering group (steering committee, project board): Group of people, chaired by the project sponsor and representing the standing organization, accountable for the project and for directing the project manager.

Sunk costs: Costs already spent on a project, not to be included in the current business case (the trade-off for further investments should exclude sunk costs and be based on costs to be made, benefits to be realized and current risk).

Supplier: A person or organization responsible for the supply of the project's deliverable(s). This implies anyone working on the creation, development and implementation of the deliverable(s).

Supplier assurance: Project assurance on behalf of the senior supplier.

Threat: A risk that would have a negative effect on one or more project objectives.

Time-boxing: Doing what can be done within a certain amount of time instead of focusing on a predefined deliverable.

Tolerance: The permissible deviation above and below the plan's target for time, cost, quality, scope, benefits or risk, without escalating the deviation to the steering group. Also see exception.

User: A person or organization who will use one or more of the project's deliverables in the broadest sense of the word. This implies anyone who uses, operates, manages, exploits, maintains, sells, buys, rents or inhabits (or otherwise has an interest in the functionality of) the project deliverable(s).

User assurance: Project assurance on behalf of the senior user.

Waterfall model: A sequential development process in which progress is seen as flowing steadily downwards (like a waterfall) through phases such as conception, initiation, analysis, design, construction, testing, implementation, production, maintenance.

Work breakdown structure (WBS): A hierarchical decomposition of the total scope of work to be carried out by the project team to accomplish the project objectives and create the required deliverables.

Work item: In an agile project approach: defined amount of work to be realized by the development team (in each iteration several work items can be realized).

REFERENCES

Berne, Eric (1964) *Games People Play: The psychology of human relations*, Grove Press, New York

Bradley, Gerald (2010) *Benefit Realisation Management: A practical guide to achieving benefits through change*, Gower, Farnham

Covey, Stephen (1989) *The 7 Habits of Highly Effective People: Powerful lessons in personal change*, Simon & Schuster, New York

Flyvbjerg, Bent, Bruzelius, Nils and Rothengatter, Werner (2003) *Megaprojects and Risk: An anatomy of ambition*, Cambridge University Press, Cambridge

Garland, Ross (2009) *Project Governance: A practical guide to effective project decision making*, Kogan Page, London

Goldratt, Eliyahu M (1997) *Critical Chain*, North River Press, Great Barrington

Hoogendoorn, Sander (2014) *This is Agile: Beyond the basics, beyond the hype, beyond scrum*, Dymaxicon, Sausalito

Jenner, Steve (2012) *Managing Benefits: Optimizing the return from investments*, The Stationery Office, London

Kahnemann, Daniel (2011) *Thinking, Fast and Slow*, Farrar, Straus and Giroux, New York

Kano, Noriaki (ed.) (1996) *Guide to TQM in Service Industries*, Asian Productivity Organization, Tokyo

Kniberg, Henrik (2007) *Scrum and Extreme Programming from the Trenches: How we do scrum*, C4Media, New York

Kolb, David (2015) *Experiential Learning: Experience as the source of learning and development*, 2nd edn, Prentice Hall, Upper Saddle River

Kotter, John P (1996) *Leading Change*, Harvard Business School Press, Boston

OGC – Office of Governement Commerce (2007) *Managing Successful Programmes (MSP)*, The Stationery Office, London

OGC – Office of Government Commerce (2009) *Directing Successful Projects with PRINCE2™*, The Stationery Office, London

Parkinson, C N (1958) *Parkinson's Law*, John Murray, London

Pink, Daniel H (2009) *Drive: The surprising truth about what motivates us*, Riverhead Books, New York

Pirsig, Robert (1991) *Lila*, Bantam Books, New York

PMI (2013a) *A Guide to the Project Management Body of Knowledge (PMBOK® Guide)*, 5th edn, PMI, Newtown Square

PMI (2013b) *The Standard for Program Management*, 3rd edn, PMI, Newtown Square

Sinek, Simon (2009) *Start With Why: How great leaders inspire everyone to take action*, Penguin Group, New York

Snijders, Paul, Wuttke, Thomas and Zandhuis, Anton (2013) *A Pocket Companion to PMI's PMBOK Guide*, Van Haren Publishing, Zaltbommel

Spitzer, Dean R (2007) *Transforming Performance Measurement: Rethinking the way we measure and drive organizational success*, Amacom, New York

Van Campen, Chretien (2012), *Sturen op geluk: Geluksbevordering door nationale overheden, gemeenten en publieke instellingen* (Aiming for Happiness: How national and local authorities and public sector organizations can promote happiness), The Netherlands Institute for Social Research, The Hague

Van der Molen, Michiel (2013) *Waarom doen we dit eigenlijk? De businesscase als succesfactor van projecten (Why are we Doing This? The business case as project success factor)*, 2nd edn, Van Duuren Management, Culemborg

Van der Zouwen, Tonny (2011) *Building an Evidence Based Practice to Large Scale Interventions: Towards sustainable organisational change with the whole system*, Eburon, Delft

INDEX

Note: *Italics* indicate a Checklist, Figure or Table.

CPSIA information can be obtained at www.ICGtesting.com
Printed in the USA
BVOW06s0859030915

416437BV00009B/33/P